BODY SIGNALS

BODY SIGNALS:
Healing Through Physical Intuition

A Manual by
Robert K. Dubiel

Speakers Publishing

second printing 1996

Printed in the United States of America.

Speakers Publishing
P.O. Box 13425
Chicago, IL 60613
email: zaRobert@gnn.com

ISBN 0–9648020–0–7

Contents

Acknowledgments

Many thanks for this book are due: To my friends, Alexander Poroshin and Sergei Strekalov of St. Petersburg, Russia, who pushed me to write down my ideas on paper, translated them into Russian and are publishing them in that country.

To my editor, Mary Louise Stefanic, who gave me faith in my own stylistic ability.

To Elyse Ebright and Jay Budai for photo and graphic support.

To Guy Spiro, publisher of The Monthly Aspectarian, and staff, who published several chapters of Body Signals in their wonderful magazine.

To Sharon Northern-Awyan, Gunn Hollingsworth, Kevin Krycka, T.J. O'Donnell, Ann Hoeffel and Vadim Moskalin for computer support.

To my Spirit Guides, for their continued love and support from the very beginning.

And most of all, to my Soul, for giving my body the sensitivity to channel the Body Signals system in the first place.

INTRODUCTION

<o>

How I Learned to Trust My Intuition

When I was growing up, spirituality meant religion, and religion—for me—was the antithesis of the flesh. I was raised Catholic from the age of seven, Baptist before that. My father taught me many rituals of denying the flesh through prayer and fasting. It seemed as though whenever I was having too much fun on my own, he would announce, "Let's say the rosary." That meant a solid hour of prayer on my knees. I learned to accept the suffering of the Catholic saints as holy and spiritual. One of my favorite prayers during my childhood was one to the Blessed Virgin Mary that asked for deliverance from this "vale of tears" called earth. Suffering and denial of earthly pleasures were what physical life was all about, if one wanted to be holy.

I came into my adolescence during the cultural revolution of the 1960's, but spent the years 1963–1970 in the sheltered environment of a Catholic seminary. By 1968, the year of "Humane Vitae," the Pope's message against birth control, I had fervently rejected a fundamentalist view of the Bible and of Christianity. Instead, I favored simple rituals such as the early Christians had practiced to attune themselves to the Holy Spirit in unconditional love.

Soon afterwards, reaction to all spirituality set in. I turned my back on all organized religion and embraced the pleasures of the flesh with a vengeance—not without guilt, of course. I doubted the existence of an organizing principle called God, focusing my idealism on social and political concerns, and trying to put the religious asceticism of my upbringing behind me.

At this time I considered myself a rational agnostic, using my conscious mind to make sense of the world. Aware of currents of mysticism sweeping the world, I did not identify with any particular brand. Occasionally I would be shown that a Higher Power exists, through synchronicities, epiphanies and rescues. Gradually, unconsciously, I opened my mind to the possibility of Extra Sensory Perception (ESP).

ESP can be one of the first glimmers of opening to the spiritual self. I had often had psychic experiences in times of crisis or stress as I was growing up, such as exams at school; I did not think much about my abilities at other times. I had neither a rational framework nor a support system where I could integrate my psychic abilities into daily life.

When I was twenty-three, I had the first of two hernia operations. During the surgery, I was quite surprised to find myself floating near the ceiling, looking down at my body on the operating table! This was very interesting—to be removed from my body with no loss of conscious awareness, watching the doctors gathered around the operating table. I seemed to be pure light, but I felt that I could change form at will. I made tentative attempts at creating a human light body, elongating my legs and arms. At some point I decided to float away to explore other parts of the hospital while the surgery continued. For the moment, I was glad to be free of my body. I remember thinking, "That body on the table is not me. My consciousness is here in this form of light."

While floating at the ceiling I continued examining the non-physical body that my consciousness was inhabiting. Essentially,

I seemed to be made up of interlocking strands of light. It was easy to project myself by directing my attention to a specific spot in the room. I remember wondering whether I could move through walls, and was just on the verge of attempting it when my attention was captured by a particularly good joke from one of the doctors. (Since this was my first surgery, I was surprised that the surgeons entertained each other with jokes while working—I have since found out that this is actually quite common—it helps them relax.) As the jokes became funnier and funnier, I drew closer and closer to the operating table, to hear better. Finally, after a really hilarious story, I slid back into my body and started laughing. "Tell that one again," I said, "it was really funny!" The doctors were aghast; one yelled, "Give him more gas!" This knocked me out for awhile, until I came back into my body later in the surgery and felt the pain—I then required another shot.

During my convalescence, when I had time to reflect on my out-of-body experience, I realized that I no longer felt identified with my physical body. I knew I was really Light energy, for I had been outside my body with no loss of consciousness. One of the surgeons remarked that the hernia had been "horrendous." I inferred that I could have easily died because of it and began to consider why this had not happened, why death had spared me. Intuitively, the inner conviction arose that I was here on earth to help people develop their ESP. This conviction took hold of me and propelled me to search for a system that would enable me to develop my own psychic skills, so that I could teach others to do the same.

During my search I remembered my common trance state during school exams when I would intuitively read the mind of the teacher and know exactly what kind of answer he or she wanted. At the time I was sure that everyone had this type of intuition and wondered why they didn't use it. My attempts to discuss intuitive exam-taking with my classmates provoked only raised eyebrows, so I had learned to keep my intuition to myself and shut it off from my everyday life. Now, determined to re-integrate it, I first considered witchcraft, but rejected it as too controlling of others. I now understand that I was tuning into other lifetimes in which I'd worked with the negative side of Magic.

I decided that my purpose in this lifetime was to free people, not enslave them, and so I left magic behind until I could have more trust in the purity of my motives.

About six months after my near-death experience, my psychic education began. A friend pointed out a newspaper article which reported that a group called The Inner Peace Movement was in town to lecture on and provide demonstrations of ESP. In the interview the lecturer gave examples of the unconscious use of psychic sensitivity, such as picking up on other people's thoughts when shopping in the supermarket. As a result one walked out of the market with many more purchases than intended. This had happened to me many times—I was intrigued. However, there was a small fee for the class, which made me skeptical about the motives of the presenters. The thought came to me that they were just out for our money. I had opened my mouth to argue this point with my friend, when a voice boomed inside my head, "Say you'll go to the lecture!" This was not my usual thinking voice; it spoke with such authority that I blurted out to my friend, "Let's go Friday!" My life has not been the same since.

That first lecture/demonstration taught me many important things about the field of energy around the body (commonly known as the aura). I learned how to see it, feel it and clean it. The first tech- nique we were taught that night entailed rubbing our hands together to bring energy to the surface of the body, the better to feel it. My forcefield felt tingly and warm; some others in the audience felt cool- ness. In addition to techniques for developing sensitivity, the presenter also gave us a basic philosophic outline called "Man and the Universe." The message in the program that impressed me most was a quote from Inner Peace Movement founder Francisco Coll, "You **ARE** a soul; you **HAVE** a body." This confirmed my feelings about my out-of-body experience (OOBE) in the hospital. During the introductory lecture that night, I made a pact with myself to seek training, with the even- tual goal of sharing these principles with others. I wanted to do what the lecturer was doing.

For the next six years this group provided me with paths to increase my spiritual sensitivity, and the training and experience to pass it on to others. I learned to cleanse my energy field, see auras, work with Spirit Guides and to pick up psychic impressions at will. In the context of Body Signals, the most striking thing about this training was that it taught me to physicalize my intuition. I learned to make strokes over my body to center myself, and to use my body as a pendulum to receive answers to questions I would ask myself. My Spirit Guides began to communicate with me through goosebumps (vibrations) on particular parts of the body, such as the spine, the top of the head or an arm.

Rarely had I experienced goosebumps before starting to practice with these techniques. Suddenly, the "chills" became an everyday occurrence. I was as if I had given my body permission to activate its higher frequencies, to expand the range of its sensitivity. Chills and goosebumps would often come in response to a thought, an idea or even an overheard remark! I was taught that they were confirmations from my Spirit Guides.

As I began to trust my inner voice as an expression of higher consciousness, the voice became more active. In addition, my ears would ring frequently and I would see lights in my field of vision. I considered these phenomena as signs that Spirit was working actively in my life. I came to view my body as a communication bridge between physical and non-physical dimensions.

—◀o▶—

As time went on, I moved away from organized groups. Nevertheless, I continued to deepen my spiritual practices in conjunction with physical awareness. The technique of self-hypnosis furthered my development considerably. I learned it as a friend used guided imagery to take us both into the Great Pyramid of Giza. He first counted up to thirty-two in order to induce a deep level of relaxation. By the time he reached twenty my body was totally paralyzed, but because I trusted him I was not afraid. When the meditation was over and he was counting down from thirty-two to one, I was able to come out of the paralysis myself. I understood that this was a useful technique to induce a deep level of concentration. I began using it in my own meditations and during the psychic readings I gave to others. After a few days of practice, counting up to twenty was enough to propel me into a state of paralysis on the left side of my body. Soon I needed to count only to ten; then five; then three. Finally this state of intense focus was available to me at will.

During self-hypnosis I was unable to move my left arm or my legs for the duration of the channeling or meditation. When I no longer needed to be in this state of consciousness, I recovered movement in my hands and feet with no ill effects. Through self-hypnosis I enhanced my ability to focus my awareness. Whether the object was a client, a tree or universal consciousness, I was able to merge with it with clarity and purpose.

After practicing for a few weeks, I discovered a new element in my body awareness. I would feel tingling in my hands and fingers when they were paralyzed, especially when I was speaking with a client. The vibrations felt like a form of confirmation or validation of the message I was receiving intuitively. I felt that these sensations were a kind of code from my Spirit Guides, but the meaning remained a mystery. My perception of these sensations seemed to stem from the Egyptian meditation I had experienced with my friend. It was after this experience of pyramid energy that my power of concentration increased to a self-hypnotic level. Since then I have regressed in meditation back to a lifetime as an Egyptian healer, in which the use of the Body Signals system was integrated into the healing practice of my temple.

One day during personal meditation I asked my Guides to explain my hand sensations. I wrote their response as follows: Vibrations in the little finger indicate truth. The ring finger—empathy or heart bonds; the middle finger—healing; the forefinger—creativity; the thumb—joy. They said that this code applies to both the left and the right hands.

This code provided a system of validation for intuitive perceptions arising from my inner self. The feeling of buzzing in the little finger, whether mine or my client's, would confirm my psychic impression if I needed substantiation for it, or feared that it was unfounded. I found that when I trusted the body signals, my clients would later validate what I had said.

I began teaching this system of psychic hand signals in Russia in 1989. It had become clear to me that this form of physicalized intuition could be a useful tool for others as well as for me, and that it was possible to teach it to them. In sharing this system I have found that hand signals help many people to increase their sensitivity to their own bodies, validate their hunches and develop their own communication system for inner guidance. I do not feel that I have invented this system; I have channeled it into this present time from ancient Egypt and beyond. My inner guidance has indicated that this system of physicalized intuition is associated with a healing vibration originating in the Pleiades constellation. The time is now right to share it with the current mass consciousness of our planet.

CHAPTER ONE

◄○►

Body Intuition
in Theory and Practice

Body signals from the intuitive level of Self are a basic channel for communicating with one's inner truth. The human body can experience a variety of distinct physical signals:

1) Arm, hand, or spine movements acting as a pendulum to obtain "yes," "no" and "neutral" answers from the unconscious. (See Chapter 5.)
2) Ringing in the ears.
3) Flashes of light in the periphery of vision.
4) Spontaneous tears.
5) "Quickening of the flesh"—sensations of tingling, heat or coolness; also called goosebumps or chills.

6) Itching on the nose, face and other parts of the skin.
7) Electrical, shock-like impulses running up the legs.
8) Paralysis during hypnotic states, especially on the left side of the body.
9) Feelings of pressure in physical energy vortices (e.g., *chakras*) as they are activated.
10) Vibrations or prickles on the hands and wrists.

The human body can be a veritable hotbed of information through sensation!

Interpretation as Context

Users of the Body Signals system have reported that most of the time body signals feel pleasant, but may be painful on occasion. There are two types of body signal pain: Activating and constricting. Activating pain occurs when energetic expansion is taking place through a field of resistance—for example, when one is committed to working through a block but still has residual attachment to the old pattern. The body signal will then be felt as a "growing pain," as though an opening is being created in the body for new energy to flow in. In this context a discomfort in the chest (heart center) might indicate that a person is expanding old beliefs about giving and receiving love.

Constricting pain feels like the energy is turning in on itself or shutting down. This may be the result of reluctance to face a truth which the unconscious wants us to be aware of. One may feel a constriction in the chest when being judgmental of someone—judgment is a form of closing the heart. I have felt constriction in my right shoulder (associated in my Kabbalistic system with mercy) while I was procrastinating on an action needed to expand my life circumstances, such as buying a car so that I could travel easily to metaphysical centers throughout the country.

In Chapter 2 we will discuss activating and constricting sensations as they relate to specific body signals in the hands.

In the Body Signals system, each intuitive signal has both a general meaning which applies to most users of the system, and a specific meaning which applies to the individual user. In addition, the sensation may heighten awareness of opportunities existing in the situation at hand, or may be a specific piece of advice good for this moment only. Let's consider the hand signal for immediate action—buzzing in this hand point may be a push to become more active *in general*, or may be a message from the unconscious to DO IT NOW! (the specific thing being considered). With practice we learn to discern the meaning of a body sensation from the context of our situation.

The three most common body signals for most people are:

- Ringing in the ears.
- Lights in the field of vision.
- "Quickening of the flesh," also known as goosebumps or chills.

Bells and Lights

Ringing in the ears and lights in the field of vision are really both manifestations of the same phenomenon—one an auditory expression, one visual. They communicate a message from the nonphysical portions of our being through physical vibrations. These signals are connecting links between our soul, our belief systems and our human personality. My use of the word *soul* here is somewhat different from its meaning in the context of Western religion. By soul I mean the expanded self, including the nonphysical portions of self, which the psychologist Carl Jung called the *numen*. The numen is in touch with the life purpose of its human personality.

Body signals can occur for two main reasons: First, to remind a person of true essence, or core self; second, to confirm or validate a thought or feeling, which may either originate internally or come from the individual's environment.

Let's consider ringing in the ears—an expression of our sense of inner hearing. Often this auditory signal sounds like a high-pitched frequency within the ear; with closer attention we may hear it as a harmonic, that is, as several pitches blended together compatibly. This harmonic may be considered as the sound frequency of the soul, or as its attempt to establish a vibration of centeredness within the body. When we have stayed a long time in a loud, crowded place, we may notice a ringing in the ears when we leave. Our vibration has gotten off-kilter from too much bombardment by confusing and incompatible energy patterns from music or from other people. The ringing in the ears is our soul's attempt to restore balance to our energy field, by making us conscious of our own unique vibration.

Our inner wisdom may give us ringing in the ears to make a specific point and get our attention. What is being said or done around us may act as an environmental stimulus that triggers the auditory mechanism. The ringing confirms or validates something that we either already know, or need to be aware of and pay attention to.

Over the years I have had many experiences of ringing in my ears, but one still reverberates in my memory. I was having dinner with a friend who was having difficulty writing a book. I suggested that she try inspirational writing with her Spirit Guides at least thirty minutes a day—to let them write through her. As I said this the ringing in my ears became so loud that it drowned out all other voices, even my own! Obviously my own Spirit Guides were making sure I followed my own advice.

This centering vibration in the ears is always available if we take the time to tune in and find it. It is our homing device for inner balance —remember that the ears help the body find a state of equilibrium. Ringing in the ears can propel us into a feeling of balance on both physical and nonphysical levels, a state in which we understand clearly what is true for us and what is not. We will "walk our talk" as the inner hearing vibration puts us in touch with our own inner truth.

Lights in the field of vision correspond to the auditory signal of ringing in the ears. When this phenomenon occurs, we usually see points of light in our visual periphery. When we turn to look at the light straight on, it will usually disappear. Sometimes, however, the light will remain, blinking merrily at us, or emanating a strong peaceful knowingness.

Our inner guidance often gives visual signals to indicate the presence of a consciousness which is "overlighting" the situation. Many sensitives have grown used to lights and auras as part of their everyday attunement experience. Occasionally the flashes of light can be dramatic, but they are usually a subtle confirmation that what we are thinking, doing or saying is in alignment with a larger picture. They are a reminder from the soul that we are never alone, that we coexist with nonphysical levels of consciousness. Separation from the Source is an illusion.

Chills

We have probably felt chills or goosebumps during a particularly scary horror movie; they can be a form of adrenaline rush, an indication of heightened awareness caused by fear. Chills can also be caused by the body's coming into contact with a vibration faster than its own. The result: Goosebumps, or what the Bible calls "the quickening of the flesh." Despite the common name "chills," the actual sensations may run from hot to cold, depending on the person and the situation.

Chills are a form of kinesthetic attunement, like ringing in the ears and lights in the field of vision. They may come on unexpectedly and may be unwelcome because of this. Once we relax into them, however, the sensations are usually pleasant—a form of heightening of the senses. We might feel chills while walking down the street or having a casual conversation. They may wash over the body with no outside stimulus at all. They may be a direct message from our soul to pay more attention to what we are doing, or to our environment in general. The catalyst for chills may be our own thought, a remark from someone else, a visual stimulus such as television, a billboard...the list of triggers is endless. Listening to our favorite piece of music or watching a beautiful sunset may trigger a flood of chills.

Like ringing in the ears, chills are a balancing and centering device to poise our energy in its own frequency. The oscillation of our life force shifts as it flows through the body; this is felt as tingling, chills, heat or pressure. We will usually experience these sensations on the surface of the skin, but sometimes we'll feel the vibrations deep in our bones.

Like other body signals, chills can validate or confirm something we suspect is true. They can indicate that we should pay attention to the stimulus and accept its truth for us in the moment. With a welcoming attitude on our part, chills will happen more frequently as we relax and breathe into them and no longer fear them as the "unexplained." They may or may not be accompanied by another body signal. We may treat all body signals as a kind of threshold, marking the transition from one state of consciousness to another.

Chills remind me that I am connected to a greater plan, a larger purpose. I remember a time some years ago when I was feeling very despondent and frustrated about my work in metaphysics. I wanted to give up metaphysical teaching and live a "normal" life. One evening while on the road giving lectures and workshops, I lay down on the bed in my hotel room to regroup my energy. As I let my body relax, I felt powerful chills wash over me in waves, especially on the five points of the body where I usually contacted my Spirit Guides. I experienced the presence of my Guides as intense but loving waves of energy swirling in and through my body. I felt completely buoyed up by their love, like one big goosebump for about an hour as they enfolded me.

That night I recommitted myself to the message of higher consciousness. Within a matter of months I left the group I had been working for and found my own voice creating and teaching my own workshops on spiritual development. The experience of letting the vibrations of love and caring into my body gave me the strength to go on to my next level of growth. I knew on a cellular level that I was not alone. I realized that I had all the backing I needed to achieve my purpose in life.

Kinesthetic Intuition

Learning to open to and trust body signals can be a way of opening to intuition on a physical level. People may feel these signals when they identify with the part of themselves that is all-knowing, see the big picture with understanding and feel one with all things. We can call this part of the psyche the inner self. Body signals can also come from the part of our unconscious which we may call the inner child. (See Chapter 4.) The inner child retains the memory of all our experiences throughout time, both pleasant and unpleasant, both in this incarnation and in other lifetimes.

These supra-rational parts of the self are meant to augment the decision-making capabilities of our conscious mind. As we get used to the idea that we are connected to all things and that anything can be a catalyst to bring on body signals, we will look to our environment to provide clues to the meaning of our lives. As a result we will be less judgmental, because we will view everything as a potential for Divine Source information.

In the context of the Michael teaching (*cf., Messages from Michael* by Chelsea Quinn Yarbro), we may say that body signals arise from the instinctual center of the psyche. The instinctual center is a neutral gear which binds together the action, intellectual and emotional centers of the psyche. The action centers relate to physical stamina and sex; the intellectual centers bring knowledge of boundaries and facts; the emotional centers motivate expression through relationship. Ideally, all three types of centers will be working in each life situation, producing well-rounded results.

As an expression of the neutral gear of instinctual center, body signals enable us to move comfortably from one center to another. For example, by paying attention to our body signals, we know whether we need more information about a situation (intellectual center), whether we should express our truth in joy and love (emotional center) or whether we need to take positive steps to reach our goals (action center).

Following our instincts through body signals puts us solidly in our essence; from there we can fan out into the intellectual, emotional and action centers of life. Our physicalized intuition will direct us according to our beliefs about life. As our true inner values get confirmation from the world around us, we will grow more confident of our inner truth and more willing to express it back to the world. The process is circular: Signals come from the world to the body and thence to the conscious mind. We then project ourselves consciously back to the world as co-creators of our reality. This is a form of the Divine Spiral of creation: Implosion and explosion; focus and expansion; death and rebirth.

Pressure and Self-Protection

We usually think of pressure as something to be avoided whenever possible, or as an unavoidable component of fast-paced urban life. However, pressure can also be a signal from higher consciousness— the progressive merger between the conscious mind and the higher self can be felt as pressure at the top of the head. In addition, when an individual is opening the aura to channeling (merger with nonphysical entities), it is common to feel one's head being jerked backwards and held in that position for the duration of the meditation. At first, this experience may seem fearful, a unfamiliar form of losing control.

Often we are quick to judge psychic experiences which feel out of the ordinary, fearing them as a prelude to unwelcome possession by negative spirits. We ignore the practice of many cultures, such as Haiti and Bali, which invite spirit possession as a form of worship of the unseen, a sort of homage by the physical plane to the spiritual. If we are unwilling to see, feel and hear the nonphysical portions of ourselves, we limit the range of our experiences to predictable, familiar ruts.

Nevertheless, self-protection is important when doing psychic work. How can we protect ourselves while opening our psychic sensitivity? The best way seems to strengthen our ability to feel our own energy flow. As we consciously circulate energy through our body, we will be able to tell the difference between pressure from negative entities and the pressure from our soul which pushes us into ecstasy. The more aware we are of how our own energy pattern feels, the better we will be able to discern what we need in life, and what we would be better off without.

Many psychic practitioners surround themselves with white or indigo light before doing psychic work. One may also surround one's body or environment with a bubble of light, love or peace. Properly used, these techniques create a shield of protection around the practitioner which admits only love or positive energies into the aura. Ideally the practitioner's aura remains permeable; that is, not all energies from outside are blocked, only negative ones.

How do you know that the shield is working? You will feel a sense of peace and protection surrounding your body or environment— negative feedback will seem to bounce off with no ill effects. Of course, you must be at peace on the inside in order for the bubble of protection to work. Otherwise, since like attracts like, you will continue to attract confusion no matter what rituals you perform. If you don't feel capable of creating the shield of protection yourself, use prayer to let the power of the Universal Life Force flow through you.

Making Body Signals a Part of Daily Life

The Spirit Guide Tien Tsing of the Council has channeled the following information on establishing a favorable psychic climate for the experience of body signals:

> *There is a web of energy cords extending from our solar plexus, from which we create our reality and are connected to our environment. When we acknowledge this psychic framework, we can draw in pertinent information as needed. In the old days it would be said that our guardian spirits were protecting us and feeding us information.*

> *How does the information travel to us? Through these cords, or bands, of energy. It is up to us, first of all, to relax the tension and anxiety which exists in our energy field, since tension will block or distort information coming in, It is possible to work under tremendous pressure, yet stay relaxed, if we are centered in our own energy bubble with all of our information lines working. Getting into the habit of attuning to this information through our bodies provides us ongoing, tangible proof that we are connected to a larger Source.*

How to open up our auric channels? The following are some move-ment techniques which create opening in the human energy field:

1) **Arms:** *Stand up, shake out your legs and arms. Find the direction where your arms want to glide effort-lessly—the path of least resistance. Take this path — that is, allow your arm to move in this arc or these arcs. Establish a regular repetition, but maintain con-trol over your movement. At some point, allow a new path to emerge—that is, allow your arms to find a dif-ferent direction and arc of movement. Do these move-ments until effort and heaviness replace lightness and effortlessness. (This technique will be useful in mas-tering the "Yes and No" technique in Chapter 5.)*

2) **Legs:** *Lie down on your back. Lift one leg at a time. This movement is more subtle than your previous arm movements. The key is in small but effortless move-ments. Find an arc of energy and glide along it. Now lower your legs, hold both of them still and feel your arc of raised movements astrally. That is, feel your nonphysical legs moving in a regular arc above your body. Then return the energy into your physical legs.*

3) **Breath:** *Use this visualization to help establish an energy ebb and flow throughout the body. Breathe in —imagine all your fibers of energy (as Castaneda would say) coalescing in a point in your solar plexus, just below your rib cage. Breathe out—let the fibers expand to fill your body, every cell, with light. Breathe in again—expand your light fibers beyond your physical body, to fill the space around it. Keep expanding and contracting to make your energy com-pact and then produce an astral density with it. That is, you are filling first your own body and then the*

psychic environment around it, with your own unique vibration. When you have breathed in this way for awhile, you will feel a fullness, as though you are larger than the capsule of your physical body.

There are many other techniques you can play with to enhance your awareness of and connection to your energy envelope, or psychic field. Experiment! Affirm to yourself, "I live in a safe universe, and only good comes to me."

◄○►

Let's take Tien Tsing's advice to heart. As we go through daily life, what are some ways we can increase our sensitivity to intuition in the body? First of all, we can pay more attention to our body's reactions to our own thoughts and emotions. Next, we will notice how we physically react to the environmental stimuli around us. Third, when the sensations occur, we can practice staying relaxed (instead of thinking, "Oh, my God, what's this tingling on my head? Am I sick?"). We can breathe into the sensations without tensing up. It is good to breathe consciously and deliberately, allowing the body signal to run its course and give its full message without being suppressed. By staying relaxed, we allow the signals to be integrated into our overall consciousness, and their lessons become part of us.

The next time you want to scratch that persistent itch in your left cheek, why not breathe into it instead? Let it deliver its information to you, consciously or unconsciously. As you realize the significance of the itch, it will help you to feel more connected with your environment. As you feel more connected to the world around you, other body signals will surface, giving insight into life circumstances that have been puzzling you.

Free Association and Intuition

My Spirit Guide Li has a message about developing sensitivity to body signals.

Body signals are a way of accessing your environment which is different from the way generally used by the conscious mind. There are many realms of available information which do not depend on rational thought. Nevertheless, once the information becomes conscious it can be picked up by the mind and correlated with already existing information. This is done through the processes of inference and free association. A stream of consciousness meditation will yield fruitful results, if you pay attention to your body signals while doing so.

To use free association, we free up our minds and allow our thoughts and feelings to connect without any prior plan. As we feel the fabric of our thoughts and feelings, we notice the patterns of sensations in the body.

Let's take Li's suggestion and do a brief meditation using the technique of free association. I would suggest that you tape record the following instructions.

First, get into a comfortable position. Breathe deeply, relaxing on the exhalation. Feel your body relax, draining tension down out the feet, through the earth and out the other side into the cosmos.

Next, allow a thought to come into your mind. Hold it there. Breathe into it. Now allow another thought to enter and interact with the first thought. Perhaps the second thought displaces the first, perhaps their interaction gives rise to a third thought. Continue to breathe deeply.

Let the focus of your thoughts change from one to another, smoothly and gently. Notice the sensations you feel in your body. As you breathe deeply and allow the panoply of your thoughts to evolve and shift, you will notice a pattern of response in your body. At some point you may feel that your thoughts are responding to your sensations—your body has then taken the lead in the free association process.

Continue with the free association of thoughts and body sensations, traveling deeper and deeper into the psyche. Eventually you will reach a thought or body sensation that wants your attention. Breathe into it and focus on it, asking it to reveal its truth to you. You are at peace.

When your body nudges you to come out of the meditation, you will feel fully awake and refreshed. Move your body and stretch. You will remember the essence of the integration you have just experienced.

Beliefs and Sensitivity

Many searchers have spent a great deal of time and energy searching for absolute truth, or a system that "has all the answers." Body Signals is not such a system. The responses we get from our unconscious mind will be colored by the issues we are working on in our lives. These in turn arise from the beliefs about life that we hold, both conscious and unconscious.

For example, if a person is learning lessons about independence, he or she will probably attract life experiences that either support or challenge self-image and self-esteem. Within the context of these life lessons it is unlikely that the person would concentrate on the truth that we are all connected, and that separation is an illusion. Instead, the individual is likely to focus on circumstances that strengthen a sense of personal identity. The body signals that the person experiences will also mirror the drive for independence, underscoring a sense of uniqueness. This is necessary, but it is not the whole picture. Body signals are reflecting the person's current state of consciousness, awareness and interests.

Awareness of body signals will lead to a conscious clarity about our beliefs about reality. We can then choose either to strengthen these beliefs, or to let them evolve into beliefs that are more appropriate to our current life lessons.

A good way to develop a more open attitude about feeling intuition in the body, is to change the belief about a "cold, cruel world" that cannot be trusted. With effort, we can replace this belief; one way is through the use of an affirmation (a positive statement about **one's personal reality**), such as the one quoted by Tien Tsing above: I live in a safe universe (from the Spirit Guide Seth, in *The Nature of Personal Reality* by Jane Roberts). Affirmations, accompanied by a real focus of our attention, will help to loosen the grip of distrust between the ego, the body and the environment. We will enjoy a more open flow between these elements of the psyche while basking in the warm glow of safety in our personal space. If the evidence in our environment does not support the notion of personal safety, it may be helpful to work with the inner child to find ways to nurture ourselves on a consistent basis. (See Chapter 4.) It takes time to establish a space of personal safety, but this is essential in order to create a positive reality for ourselves.

Meditation to Feel the Life Force

Let's put physicalized intuition into practice with the following meditation. I suggest you ask a friend to take you through this.

Let's put physicalized intuition into practice with the following meditation. I suggest you ask a friend to take you through this.

1) Get comfortable and relaxed, using slow, deep, connected breaths.
2) Instruct yourself to let go completely on the exhalation.
3) Close your eyes.
4) Imagine a column of light coming through the energy center at the top of your head. The column can be any color that feels good to you.
5) See the light flow in through the top your head, down through your body and out your feet.
6) Now use your breath to inhale the light into the top of your head, exhaling it out your feet.

Gradually during this meditation you will feel a pathway of energy opening up in your body. The energy makes you feel alive on a deep cellular level, yet also relaxed. Now you can open up safely to a greater degree of life force inside your body. Let this life force go where it is needed most—whether it be your heart, your stomach or another part of the body. Feel a stream of light from the universe entering this part of your body while you inhale. The light becomes part of your body as you exhale.

Now connect the top of your head with the enlightened part of your body, using your breath to create a pathway between these two points. With every breath this pathway becomes stronger. You can use it in your daily life to send yourself energy whenever it feels appropriate.

Notice how this energy feels as it travels down the pathway. Is it strong or subtle? Intense or gentle? Is it cool or warm? A pressure or a feeling of lightness?

When you feel you have experienced the light energy enough for now, send it down to your feet and out into the earth. Now open your eyes and stretch. Roll around in the stretch, feeling the delightful life force enlivening every cell of your body!

◄o►

This chapter has introduced concepts of energy flow between the body and its environment, both physical and universal. The more you practice these and similar techniques, the closer you will move in your life toward bridging the gap between spirit and flesh. In this book you will have the opportunity to practice many techniques to deepen your trust in your body's instincts!

This chapter concludes with a further message from Tien Tsing of the Council:

We want you to relax as you use this system, as you get more in touch with the sensitivity in your bodies. As you relax you will find the hidden places in your psyche which yearn to be let out and run free. You will feel that you have been missing parts of yourself, but that those parts are found now.

Body signals can provide you with one more tool to use on your journey, to make sure that you are on your path and in touch with your true feelings. For you contain all the answers you will ever need, don't you? It's just that they are sometimes in unusual places—a ringing in your ears, a buzzing in your little finger. Why not? God is everyone, everywhere.

Inside Hand

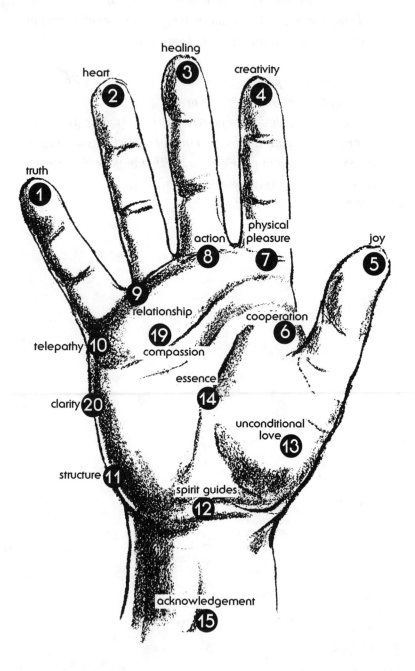

healing

heart

creativity

truth

physical
pleasure

action

joy

relationship

cooperation

telepathy

compassion

essence

clarity

unconditional
love

structure

spirit guides

acknowledgement

Outside Hand

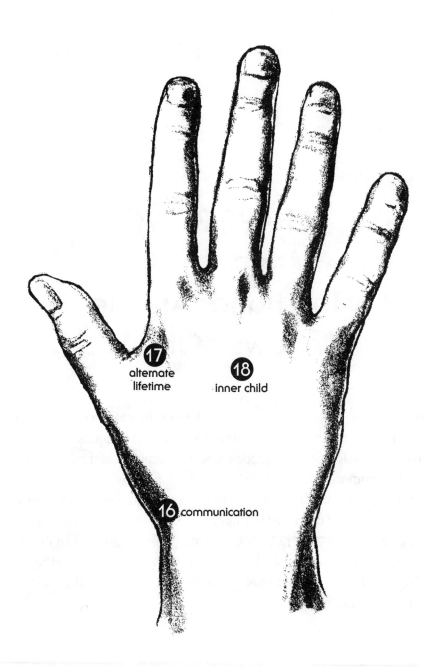

CHAPTER TWO

◄O►

The Hands Are the Windows of the Soul

The psychic code which we will explore in the next two chapters is specific to the hands. Other parts of the body also receive signals from the unconscious, but this code especially emphasizes the hands as a tool for communication with the "trans-conscious" portions of Self. Each hand point which can be used to receive signals from the inner self is listed and described in this chapter and the next, accompanied by practical illustrations for incorporating these signals into daily life. This chapter describes the body signals which can occur on the five fingers. Chapter 3 will discuss points of soul contact in other parts of the hands and wrist.

Correlation With Other Systems

Many systems of body knowledge make use of the hands to receive conscious information or to channel energy. The paradigm of acupuncture uses lines of energy called meridians to describe energy flow through the entire body, including the hands. Each meridian has been assigned a specific meaning in the Chinese acupuncture tradition. The tip of the middle finger is said to be concerned with healing through balance. The tradition of energy circulation called, in Chinese, *Ch'i Kung*, also uses the middle finger to project healing energy to other parts of the body. Numerous spiritual healing systems such as Reiki and shamanism employ laying on of hands and include techniques for channeling healing energy through them.

The art of palmistry ascribes meanings to each part of the hand. The Mound of Venus underneath the thumb is said to be concerned with matters of love. The Mound of Mars underneath the middle finger deals with drive and aggressiveness.

The code which my students and I have developed does not spring from any other system. It originated spontaneously; the sensations just started to happen in our bodies! Interpretations usually came weeks or months later. When they occurred, we did not try to match them up with other systems. The paradigm of Body Signals is a kinesthetic intuitive system which stands on its own and can be used alone, as well as in conjunction with other systems. I would welcome your feedback on how Body Signals interfaces with other systems that you use.

The Plasticity of Form

The body itself is a much more flexible paradigm than we usually consider it to be. In our Western culture we have been taught that the body is separated from Spirit. If we want to change the form of our bodies, for example, for weight loss or muscle gain, it is supposed to be hard work. The body is viewed primarily as a vehicle for locomotion or for assimilation of impressions from the outside world. Our perception of the body tends to be one or two dimensional—space oriented, but with little time perception. Yet we can observe that each part of the body is flexible in its fulfillment of different functions, depending on the needs of the situation. We can extend our hand in a gesture of friendship, to clinch a business deal or to send energy for healing. With brain damage, formerly underutilized portions of the brain compensate and start to perform needed functions. Taking a leap in intuitive logic, can we use our hand as a kind of conduit to send and receive information from the non-physical portions of Self?

The body is not merely an encasing mechanism for the soul; nor is it a prison meant to separate us from bliss. It is the physical focus of a much larger field of consciousness, or "morphogenic field," as biologist Rupert Sheldrake would term it (*cf.*, his book, *The Presence of the Past: Morphic Resonance and the Habits of Nature*). Each cell of our body focuses the consciousness and the blueprint of the organism of which it is a part. This organism includes both the physical body and the non-physical parts of Self in a field of awareness which uses time and space but also leaps across them to make needed changes in the Now.

Body Signals as a Learning System

In this book we consider the possibility of plugging ourselves into electromagnetic frequencies which are different from the "normal" band of energy that we may be used to feeling in our bodies. These frequencies which join the different parts of the Self together, are vibrationally faster than those which connect us with our outer environment. Consequently they capture a different band of information—one which includes physical data, but is not limited to it. Deeper and broader feedback is also present, coming from different parts of the Self—both from the unconscious mind, which may be portrayed by the symbol of the inner child; and from the superconscious mind, or higher self.

Accelerated learning systems and systems of relaxation such as Biofeedback are scientifically mapping the parts of the brain that we use when we are in altered states of consciousness. In accelerated learning systems the student learns to read the context and the energy field of the book or language being studied, rather than each individual word. The student then stores the information in a mental data bank for further use. Stored data is automatically put into an appropriate contextual framework—conscious recall of written and spoken material thus improves. Biofeedback is designed to teach the individual conscious control of relaxation states. The participant learns to consciously alter his/her brainwave patterns. The slower the brainwave, the more relaxed the individual and the broader the band of information that is accessible to the conscious mind.

In developing sensitivity to a particular code of intuitive signals in the body, it is beneficial to use a form of "directed non-attention"; that is, maintaining an open, receptive state of mind, while at the same time remaining alert for body awareness details. I learned a related skill some years ago while playing with dice. I was attempting to make one pattern of numbers come up consistently, 1–6, 1–6, 1–6. To do this successfully I had to hold the picture of the dice coming up 1–6 in my mind, then let the image go and look away as I threw the dice. I needed to focus my attention elsewhere in the moment in order to let the manifestation occur. This lesson was a variant of the old saying, "A watched kettle never boils." By directing our attention elsewhere, we give the non-physical portions of our being the space required to bring our conscious goal into manifestation.

In asking questions with the use of body signals it is important to maintain a relaxed emotional detachment about outcomes. As in dowsing (the practice of using a rod, often metal, to find water or to scan the environment for information), the body is used as an impartial instrument. As a result we become more aware of the information which is available on the periphery of consciousness, information which validates and enriches our experience by connecting us to our environment, both inner and outer.

The "Feel" of Hand Signals

On the hands, intuitive signals are usually felt as vibrations of varying degrees of intensity, ranging from a light tickle to complete numbness of the affected area. This variation is related in part to the importance of the information to the receiver. The strength of the sensation may also have something to do with the amount of sensitivity that the receiver has to his or her body. In other words, how strong a sensation does it take to get your attention?

In our Western culture we usually must be re-educated to feel our physical sensations: Our senses have been dulled by steady streams of drugs and painkillers that we have ingested, and by our general sense of alienation from the workings of our own bodies. In my practice of rebirthing (a form of conscious breathing), I sometimes encounter clients who say they feel nothing going on. They have difficulty focusing their attention on their bodies for a sustained period of time. Other clients may not report specific sensations; they say they feel "good," "relaxed" or "OK." Because our culture has suppressed the idea that the body is a repository of relevant information for our lives, many of us have stopped paying attention to the constant stream of signals that the body brings to the surface of awareness.

The Origin of Hand Signals

My Spirit Guide Nathan (who, by the way, touches me on my left arm) says:

> Body signals are an attempt to recapture some of the physicalized intuition which has been lost in your culture. (That is why you, Robert, don't want to use existing systems.) Your purpose is to train people to develop their own highly specialized, highly individualized form of inner guidance. As more people are consciously connected to the Source of their power, there will be a chance for conscious, concerted effort based on the real needs of both humanity and the environment. There will be a give and take between human beings and the environment, which is not now known to you. This is very important at this time, as your species enters into a conscious co-creation with the earth, as has been seen in specific societies such as Holland (dikes and dunes) and Bali (rice terraces).

In practice with Body Signals thus far, my students and I have discovered twenty signal points on each hand. However, this is not a final figure. The more this system is shared with others, the more additional points become activated. The number is unlimited. Already I and other Body Signals practitioners sometimes feel vibrations in parts of the hands where a meaning has not yet been assigned. I welcome feedback that you, the reader, may have in your experience with new body points and signals.

As recounted in the *Introduction*, I first began to work with the system of hand signals by using the five fingers. I had been feeling tingling on my fingers for some time while using self-hypnosis, especially when I was meditating or doing psychic readings for clients. I sensed that the vibrations were a code of some kind. While meditating one day I decided that I was ready to "crack the code." I asked my guides for the meanings of the hand signals and wrote down their responses. In brief, they told me that the little finger was the truth finger, the ring finger stood for heart bonds, the middle finger indicated healing, the forefinger (index finger) was concerned with creativity and that the thumb was related to joy. Buzzing in my little finger confirmed their message, of course; I felt ready to incorporate this information into my daily life.

My students and I began to experiment with this code, paying attention to the situations in which we felt vibrations on our fingers. Hand signals acted as validations for our inner knowings, intuitions and feelings. After feeling the hand signals we would often receive confirmations from the environment (people, places, things) that our intuition was correct. For example, one might have the thought, "I think I'll roll up my car windows; it will probably rain later this afternoon." At that moment the sky might be cloudless. If the little finger started buzzing as one thought about rolling up the windows, one would be more likely to pay attention to the hunch. Later, when it rained, one would feel validated. This experience would strengthen the individual's trust of body signals the next time they occurred.

As my students and I have worked with physicalized intuition we have developed more specific interpretations for the signals on each one of the five fingers. Let's consider them in turn, starting with the little finger.

Point One: Little Finger

In this system of Body Signals the little finger is the all-purpose truth finger. It can validate one's own thought. It can also confirm the thought of someone else, illustrating that the body is a telepathic receiver. Television, radio, a book, a billboard—all can give input which our bodies respond to by feeling vibrations. A piece of art or music can put us in touch with a core level of our personal truth— the little finger validates this by buzzing. Hunches, overall evaluation of a situation, irrational perceptions, doubts about what we are being told—all can be confirmed by buzzing in the little finger. These vibrations take into account our personal belief systems, which will color the information we are open to receive. When the little finger tingles, some part of us acknowledges that present circumstances are reflecting what is true for us in the moment. Our conscious mind may or may not agree with this perception coming from the unconscious.

Most of the time, users of the Body Signals system experience a tingling sensation over the surface of the skin. Some practitioners have differentiated between sensations felt on each joint of their fingers. We employ the sensations as a catalyst, a foundation of truth to build on. We find that body signals are most useful not in telling us what to do, but rather in giving us clues to go on. "Which line of action would be most productive?" "What is the real truth in the situation?" "Should I pay attention to this uneasy feeling of mistrust?" And so forth.

Case History

One day a new client, one whom I had not met previously, walked into my apartment for a private session and sat down after a brief greeting. For some reason I did not feel like making preliminary small talk to establish rapport with her. I just relaxed and closed my eyes; almost instantly I began to see images of a young man drowning.

At this moment I remembered a recent client whose friend had drowned in a swimming accident. Thinking that I was picking up irrelevant bleed-throughs from the previous reading, I tried to dismiss the images and move on. But they kept returning, becoming clearer and more vivid. I knew intuitively that the drowned man I was "see-ing" had been twenty-one years old. This was about the age of the friend of my recent client at the time of his accident. As these impressions became stronger and stronger, I had to accept that they were connected to the woman sitting in front of me. Still, I was reluc-tant to share them with her, since they were so specific and I con-sciously knew nothing about her. Then I noticed the buzzing on my little finger, the truth finger; I plucked up my courage and plunged in:

"Did you have a twenty-one year old son who drowned?"

My client's eyes opened wide and she replied, "Yes, I did. That's why I came to see you today—to find out if he's all right."

At that moment I knew that I'd accurately read the information in my client's energy field. I'd used my experience with the previous client as a springboard to scan the current situation. My body signal gave me the courage to trust my intuition. By following my hunch I established credibility with my client and helped her to do significant release work with her son that day.

—◂o▸—

There may be times when the truth finger buzzes about courses of action that are apparently contradictory. This may indicate that different aspects of truth have been reached. Or perhaps several potential paths may be taken, each of which would further our growth. We may ask ourselves, "Which course of action makes me feel the most alive?" The truth signal may be a guide to lead us deeper into the core of our true feelings, where the most effective decisions can be made and carried out.

Point Two: Ring Finger

We have discovered that the ring finger (the one next to the little fin-ger) can indicate several aspects of heart connections. In our culture one form of heart-bonding is reflected in the custom of placing the wedding ring on this finger. This symbolizes that the married couple are linked at the heart. In everyday life the ring finger could buzz to indicate an empathic bond. When we are emotionally connected to a person, it is easy to feel their feelings and to share energy with them, whether this means sharing their joy or their pain. When we feel physical pain while our heart finger is buzzing, this could be a reflection of the other person's traumas, not our own blockages.

A second common meaning of the ring finger signal is that there is a "past life" connection with another person, place or time; that is, that another incarnation of ours has "been here before." If we were walking down the streets of a foreign city and suddenly the ring finger began to buzz, it would be an indication that the place held some special meaning for us, whether in this life or in another. Sometimes we can go visiting in our sleep, and so have a sense of *deja vu* when we arrive in the actual physical situation. Our heart connection will feel especially intense in places where we have lived a rich, emotional life. When I visited the Italian cities of San Gimigniano and Sienna, I experienced this resonance on the ring finger, along with an intense aesthetic connection to the local art and architecture. Later I discovered that I'd been an artist of the Siennese school in the fourteenth century.

When we meet "new" people they will often feel familiar to us, as though we have met before. In these cases the heart finger may start to buzz. We can take this as a sign that, indeed, we do know our new acquaintance on some level. We are already connected to them at the heart—a positive connection of unconditional love. Practitioners of Body Signals often find that when the heart finger is buzzing, we and our new acquaintances treat each other as long lost friends who are just now resuming our relationship!

The ring finger can also be activated during regression work, both past life and childhood regression. The regressee often feels a persistent sensation on this finger while in the altered state of consciousness necessary for past life recall. Why? Past life memory does not originate in the conscious, rational mind; it is channeled through emotional links centered in the heart. As a past life regressionist I treat heart finger vibrations as validation that the client is really experiencing a past life or childhood memory.

Cultural Relativisim and Interpretation

What role do cultural symbols play in assigning a specific meaning to each body signal? Let's use the heart as an example. In our culture the heart is strongly associated with the emotions, as opposed to the intellect. In a different setting the ancient Egyptians spoke of the "intelligence of the heart," a kind of core intuitive wisdom. In both cultures the heart is perceived as an organ that connects us to our deeper senses, and to each other, through the feeling of compassion. The Jewish mystical tradition of the Kabbalah also confirms this interpretation of the heart center. I would say that the popular culture combines with ancient, even unconscious mystical traditions to both create and reflect the truth as we experience it in everyday life. Jung certainly addressed this issue in his book *Man and His Symbols*.

Perhaps the tradition of the wedding ring has done much to strengthen the connection of this particular finger with the heart in our culture. There may exist other cultures in which heart bonds are not associated with this finger at all. The heart itself may have a much different symbolic meaning for some peoples. There is no doubt that personal experience of reality is culturally biased. Therefore it is not wise to become dogmatic about the interpretations given in this book, considering them as the only ones possible for a vibration sensed in the body.

Point Three: Middle Finger

In this system of body signals the middle finger signifies physical healing. It indicates that the psyche is concerned with the proper circumstances and environment needed for good physical health, both for creating it and maintaining it. Let's look at an example of the middle finger in action: You feel a cold coming on; that sense of tightness and constriction is in the outer layers of your aura, moving inward toward your body. You think to yourself, "What can I do to head off this cold?" The thought occurs to you, "Drink chamomile tea and go to bed early." Concurrently you notice a tingling in your middle finger, a pleasant sensation. You can rest assured that following your impulses will contribute to your overall health and well-being. It's like having a built in doctor right in your body! The body signal will also activate if you are asking a "yes" and "no" question of your inner self in an area of life which is concerned with health and healing. (See Chapter 5.) "Would less fat intake be good for me at this time?" You might receive both a "yes" answer and feel a tingling on your middle finger at the same time.

People who channel healing energy, especially through their hands, will often feel buzzing or tingling in the middle finger when the client makes a breakthrough. Psychologists and other therapists concerned with emotional and mental healing will also feel sensations in this finger as their clients come back into balance.

Point Four: Index Finger

Buzzing on the index finger (forefinger) has several meanings: It is a signal both of prosperity and of sexuality, under the general heading of creativity. That is, the universal life force manifests both as material abundance and as new life. This correlation assists us in healing concepts about sex and material prosperity: They are both aspects of the creative flow. The forefinger signal indicates that creative energy is present around the issues of abundance and the life force. The signal validates whatever we are planning or discussing. We can trust that our project will enhance our creative expression. This could be in the areas of art, business, personal relationships or a healthy assertiveness toward life!

One of the most striking confirmations of the forefinger's connection with creativity is illustrated in Michelangelo's "The Creation" in the Sistine Chapel in Rome. In this painting Michelangelo portrays God the Father as giving Adam the gift of life by extending his right forefinger to touch Adam's left one. God is sending the life force through the forefinger of his right hand, while Adam receives it with his left hand. This illustrates the esoteric tradition of the right hand as active or sending, and the left as receptive, which will be discussed later in this chapter.

Point Five: Thumb

The "thumbs up" sign is used in many cultures as a sign of approval. In this system of body signals the thumb indicates joy. Many of us are out of touch with our core feelings and need a reminder from the unconscious about what really makes us happy. Buzzing on the thumb is a signal of this. For instance, if a friend invites you to a party, you might decline by complaining, "I have too much work to do." Then you notice that your thumb buzzes as the image of the party becomes stronger and clearer for you. It's easy then to surrender to the joy that your unconscious, through your friend, is extending to you.

Pain as a Body Signal

As mentioned in the previous chapter, ongoing sensitivity to body signals makes one aware of both painful and pleasurable sensations on the fingers. Users of this system have come to understand that signals on the hands can provide several nuances of meaning. The thumb signals joy, but its opposite—anger or rage—will come through as pain in that digit.

This was driven home to me when I was traveling with a friend in New York State. As we were driving through the Hudson Valley I was struck by its beauty and majesty. My friend had previously lived in this valley and was emotionally connected to it. We turned a bend in the road and suddenly a huge power plant loomed in front of us. "What's that?" I asked. My thumb started to throb with pain. My friend began to rage that it was a nuclear power plant, which posed a safety hazard to the valley that she loved so much. As she talked it became clear to me that the pain in my thumb was mirroring her anger. Empathically my thumb was reflecting the lack of joy in my friend's consciousness at that moment!

Through this experience, I learned that constricting pain can reflect the opposite meaning to the usual body signal. Pain in the truth finger indicates that the full truth is not being expressed or perceived in the situation. Pain in the heart finger acts as a warning that one is being judgmental or that one's actions are not coming from love. We might call this having a closed heart. Pain in the healing finger indicates that something is being done or thought about that is not good for physical health.

Pain in the forefinger signals a blockage in the flow of the creative life force. It may warn of a blockage in self-expression or communication if a contemplated course of action is carried out. If we are involved in an unhealthy relationship, pain in the forefinger may warn us to distance ourselves from that person sexually before our life force and creativity are drained away.

It has helped participants in this system to recognize that pain can be a useful signal of inner truth. With this attitude we can use pain as a teacher without judging ourselves or others. As experience with body signals has unfolded, practitioners have become aware of a second nuance of meaning for pain: Expansion of consciousness. Sometimes energy attempts to flow from the Soul consciousness through to the physical body, but encounters resistance from the ego (conscious mind). We feel pain as the Soul energy tries to find an open pathway through the body. I call this sensation "expanding pain" as opposed to the constricting pain of warnings.

When we receive a true message that we don't want to hear, we may feel pain in the little finger (truth finger). This kind of pain feels different from the warning signal which means "Not true!" Pain due to the ego's resistance feels like forced expansion in the finger, as though the energy were trying to create a larger capsule for itself. Expanding pain can be a step toward growth, as the truth is felt despite the ego's resistance. I consider it a positive signal, since we can dissolve our blocks as we breathe into them. This is in contrast to constricting pain, which signals that the energy in that part of the psyche is holding itself shut and not allowing the life force to flow through it, due to concepts, beliefs and prejudices that are no longer appropriate.

When energy is constricting in a hand point, another part of the body may feel tightness as well. One might feel pressure in the ring finger and at the same time a constriction in the center of the chest, the heart center. Both sensations would be a warning that the heart center is shutting down. We would not be open to send or receive love.

Interpreting Physical Intuition

Two factors are important in order to interpret body signals effectively: One is practice, and the other, the realization that body signals are contextual. They are reflections from our psychic environment, influenced by our beliefs about life. Generally, body signals do not mirror absolute truth, but rather truth as it is experienced by the individual psyche with its own beliefs, strengths and weaknesses.

With practice our sensitivity will expand so that we can discern shades of meaning in each hand point. For example, we might ask ourselves, "Does this pain in my little finger mean that I am telling myself a lie? Or perhaps I am hearing the truth and resisting it?" The end result of this level of discernment will be a conscious cooperation with our Soul's blueprint for our lives, due to greater awareness of opportunities for growth.

Right Hand–Left Hand

For most people who have used this system, there seems to be a distinct difference in meaning between sensations in the right and left hands. Sensations in the right hand generally indicate that we are actively sending vibrations or information from our energy field (aura) to our environment. Sensations on the skin of the left hand mean that we are receiving information and energy from the environment. Note that our environment can be both internal (the psychic environment of thoughts and feelings) or external (the people, places and things around us).

There are exceptions to this rule, especially among left-handed people, where the left hand is the sender and the right the receiver. I advise you to test for yourself which of your hands sends out energy and signals, and which receives.

Once we determine which hand is sender and which receiver, we will probably notice that the meaning of each signal varies according to the hand. If the creativity finger is buzzing on your receptive hand in a place that indicates prosperity, this might be a signal to open up to the abundance that is coming your way. Or it might confirm that you are already involved in a situation which is bringing prosperity.

On the other hand, suppose that while you are considering a major purchase, you feel a buzzing on the forefinger of your sending hand. This would indicate the planned purchase is a good expression of your creative flow. Your creativity is taking the form of recirculating energy back to the universe by spending money. However, if you were to feel a constriction in the forefinger while considering the purchase, it might mean that the purchase would be ill-advised at this time, from the point of view of the best use of creative resources. If the pain is more a feeling of expansion in the finger, it might mean that your inner self really wants to make the purchase, but is encountering resistance from ego fears. It may be necessary to stop, take a deep breath and see the whole picture.

When you feel pain in your body signal points, breathe into it consciously and give your fears permission to transform when they are ready. When you feel a letting go of blockages, reconsider your decision from the point of view of essence (your core truth).

Many users of this system feel vibrations on the left hand when they are relaxed in meditation or when doing psychic counseling. These signals indicate that they are picking up truth from their inner psychic environment or from the aura of the client. When practitioners are sending energy to someone during healing or are communicating thoughts and feelings through telepathy, they may feel appropriate buzzings on the right hand, the active sender.

Over the last few years more signal points have emerged on the hands, to fine tune different aspects of information from the unconscious. In Chapter 3 we will discuss these additional points.

CHAPTER THREE

◄o►

Fourteen Additional
Hand Points

After extensive practice with the five body signals in my fingers, I began to feel vibrations in other parts of my hands as well. This occurred especially after I started teaching the Body Signals code in Russia several years ago. New signal points sometimes opened up in class, both for me and for my students. It became clear to us that I did not "own" this system. Channeling Body Signals gave me a sense of stewardship of the information, which is available to all who open their sensitivity to use the body's consciousness in a more elastic, pliable way.

Below is a list of the other hand signal points which practitioners have experienced in this system. All these points are found on the inside of the hand and wrist, unless otherwise noted. See the accompanying diagrams for clarification. The finger points (Points 1–5) have been listed already, in Chapter 2.

Point 6: Cooperation. Fold of skin between thumb and forefinger.

Point 7: Pleasure. Mound underneath forefinger.

Point 8: Immediate Action. Mound underneath the middle finger.

Point 9: Relationship. Point on the hand between ring finger and little finger.

Point 10: Telepathy. Point at the base of the little finger on the outside of the hand.

Point 11: Structure. Point where the outside of the hand meets the wrist.

Point 12: Spirit Guide. The middle bottom of the hand, just above the wrist.

Point 13: Unconditional Love. The Mound of Venus underneath the thumb.

Point 14: Essence. The center of the palm.

Point 15: Acknowledgment. The center of the inside wrist.

Point 16: Communication. The outside of the wrist underneath the thumb.

Point 17: Alternate Reality. The back of the hand, underneath the Cooperation Point.

Point 18: Inner Child. The middle of the back of the hand.

Point 19: Compassion. Palm, between Relationship and Essense Points.

Description of Hand Points

Point 6: Cooperation. Fold of skin between thumb and forefinger.

This point is the bridge between creativity (forefinger) and joy (thumb), effected through cooperation with others. The Cooperation Point can signal the desirability of making agreements and contracts. On the left hand, buzzing in the Cooperation Point means that the situation is signaling us that there is energy available for agreements and contracts. On the right hand, buzzing means that we are sending out an active energy of cooperation into our situation or environment.

As discussed in the previous chapter, constricting pain in the left hand Cooperation Point signifies that there is some blockage present which prevents agreements from coalescing. No matter how willing and eager all parties appear, obstruction is present on some level. On the other hand, if we feel a pain in our right hand Cooperation Point, we are the ones holding things up when they could be flowing smoothly.

Body Signals practitioners often feel the Cooperation Point buzzing when they are involved with group energy of a healing or meditative nature. The Cooperation Point may also signal that several parts of the psyche are working together to create harmony within—the inner child, the conscious mind and Spirit Guides, for example, or the shadow self and the anima/animus.

Point 7: Physical Pleasure, eroticism, sensuality, celebration of the physical. Mound underneath forefinger.

My Spirit Guides say:

> *Sensual pleasure is the term we want to use for this hand point, because it connotes an **active embracing** of Divine Love.*

In this context pleasure involves the creation of space for expressions of love and sensuality in the body. On the physical plane, love always includes merger in some form, whether physical or energetic, an energy exchange between people, plants or parts of the psyche.

Through this energy exchange we remember that separation is illusion. Sensual pleasure is a way for our cells to truly understand unconditional love through celebrating Self!

The erotic is not always connected to the intellectual or even the emotional centers, but it is definitely connected to our creative centers. When erotic energy is allowed to be expressed in an unimpeded way, it sets up a creative resonance which builds its own momentum. Then the creativity can be used in any endeavor we choose. When we are "living on love," a condition in which we do not need food or sleep, we embody the erotic principle in two ways: First, we generate an endless flow of tangible energy from within (what the Chinese call "ching"); this energy is denser and more corporeal than usual thought energy. Next, we direct this energy to fuel our creative projects with charisma (that glow you see around "sexy" or creative people).

When we allow ourselves to blend energies with another person, even without touching (remember the movie, "Cocoon"?), we activate our erotic frequencies and can achieve soul union. The support we feel from such a soul merger can fuel our creative expression in all areas of life, as our inner child feels the security that "somebody loves me."

By actively loving our physical body for its own sake, just as it is, because it is a focused expression of God's beauty, or a "temple of the Holy Spirit," we will often find our Pleasure Point buzzing. We can celebrate our physicality in a variety of ways: Giving or receiving a sensuous massage; conscious circulation of the life force ("chi") energy throughout the body, actively directing our life force; taking a hot bath; running into the wind on the beach or relaxing in a favorite chair. When we let the tension drain out of our bodies and siphon out into the earth (a process which transmutes it into usable creative energy for the earth), we merge with our environment—with the hot tub, the massage table, the sand, the chair. As we let go and allow ourselves to feel the union, we are refreshed.

Point 8: Immediate Action. Mound underneath middle finger.

Vibrations on this point indicate that immediate action is warranted. In palmistry this mound is known as the Mound of Mars, which rules aggression. This point is connected to the healing finger, which is concerned with rebalancing. The Action Point underneath this finger starts buzzing when rebalancing is needed **NOW!** The spiritual teacher Francisco Coll speaks of "the healing that comes with accomplishment." That is what we feel when we act on the immediate impulse of this hand point.

My Spirit Guide Ariana says,

> *It is not always enough to breathe consciously—sometimes you must **ACT**. Truth in life consists both in knowing the truth and acting upon it.*

Feeling the buzzing of the Immediate Action point is an opportunity to seize the moment for our own good. This body signal is not an indicator of outside pressure to do something, but rather an invitation to go with our own inner flow. One evening during a Body Signals class a student felt her Immediate Action point buzzing. Tuning into what it meant, she received the inner guidance to leave the class at once, go home and get some sleep—she was exhausted. She did not follow this advice and was groggy and uncommunicative for the rest of the evening.

Point 9: Relationship Point. Fold of skin on the palm between the ring finger and the little finger.

As with the fold of skin referred to above as the Cooperation Point, the Relationship Point acts as a bridge between two distinct vibrations: Truth (little finger) and Empathy (ring finger). The Relationship Point is activated when two or more people are forging agreements with each other, which connects their solar plexuses with psychic cords of energy.

Here are some examples of situations in which the Relationship Point could be activated: Going into business with a partner or partners; getting married or forming a common household with a lover or roommate; deciding to conceive and raise a child with your partner; revising a business agreement with a long-term client.

At first I considered this hand point to be a signal of intuitive connection to another person or to the environment. With practice,

I refined the meaning of the body signal, realizing that all body signals connect us with our intuitive nature. I shifted my perspective of this hand signal during a rather intense business meeting. I was visiting a new holistic center in my area, meeting the proprietors and signing contracts to teach classes, do psychic fairs and workshops there over a period of several months. Our negotiations were extensive—the meeting lasted three hours. As it was coming to a close, the fold of skin between the ring finger and little finger started to vibrate strongly. I understood at that moment that my body was signaling the start of an ongoing relationship between me and the center. I was now part of it. The contracts I had signed were not empty pieces of paper—they were outward signs of a psychic link that had been established between me and the center. This signal reminded me that we all inhabit a shared psychic space when we make agreements with others.

The Relationship Point provides confirmation of the psychic reality of contracts, both personal and legal. Breaking the contract may be necessary at some point, but it is important to acknowledge the resulting psychic consequences and energy shifts. As we activate our Relationship Hand Point, we will become more conscious of the ramifications of our choices.

Point 10: Telepathy. Outside of the hand, just below the little finger.

We may define intuition as an inner knowing, coming from transphysical centers of perception (inner radar). Telepathy could be called the aspect of intuition which actively reads people, places and things, using the associative power of the mind as a springboard. ("Hmm. This sky reminds me of that time when I fell off the horse when I was four. My cousin Darlene washed my ear then—I wonder how she's doing?" You arrive home to find a message from Darlene on your answering machine.)

The *ajna chakra* (third eye), located above the bridge of the nose in the lower forehead, is the part of the body traditionally associated with telepathic ability. The third eye can both give and receive mental messages. When our powers of telepathy are opening, we may feel a pressure in our forehead as well as in the Telepathy Point on the hand.

Notice when these body points are buzzing, whether your forehead feels hot or cool; pressure or lightness; a feeling of expansion in the third eye while your inner pictures are becoming more vivid. Are you picking up on the thoughts of others while you feel these signals, or is your sense of synchronicity (correlated timing) heightened?

At the age of four, I experienced a telepathic sensitivity quite common in children of that age (*cf.*, *The Magical Child* by Joseph Chilton Pearce). I began to hear people's thoughts before they spoke. Often they would repeat the thought I had heard verbatim, but I became confused when they said something quite different from what I had heard inside their minds. I asked my mother, "Why do people lie?" "Why do you say that?" she replied. "Because I hear what they're thinking, and it's different from what they say." My mother was alarmed by this—I got the distinct message that "listening in" was not socially acceptable behavior. We were supposed to go along with what people said and pretend it was the truth, even if we knew otherwise! I remember resolving to myself, "When I grow up, I'm going to show people how simple life really is: Just tell the truth!"

The Telepathy Point on the hands functions as a kind of conduit through which energy can flow to produce tangible results. You can test your sensitivity by conducting experiments with your friends. Send them mental images and inner sounds. Focus your attention as well on other stimuli such as smells, tastes and tactile sensations. Think of a beautiful picture or a favorite piece of music, and then send the energy of your concentration out to your friend, the receiver. Open yourself to receive impressions from your friend as well. Notice whether you are better at sending or receiving? Do you send/receive more effectively using mental thoughts, emotional associations or sensory stimuli? Use the Telepathy Point on your hand as a barometer for your aptitude and progress.

The left hand's Telepathy Point indicates that you are psychically linked to the mind of a person, place or group. The right hand's Telepathy Point indicates that you are sending out mental signals to your environment, either consciously or unconsciously. Pain in the Telepathy Point could mean that you are resisting mental melding (left, receptive hand) or are trying to fool yourself into believing or projecting a lie (right, active hand).

Point 11: Structure Point. Organization. The outside of the hand, just above the wrist.

To organize something means to put form on it, providing structure where before there was only void or chaos (unstructured potential). The void contains all potentials within itself. Some take longer to manifest than others—some will not manifest in this reality.

As Westerners with an externally oriented value system, we tend to emphasize organization and structure, no matter where in the lifecycle of a project we may be—even if an entity (for example, person, business) is in a winding down period, we tend to try to give it new life through structure and rules. The Structure Point can be a useful indicator of when it really is time to put structure on our environment, and when it is better to leave things alone.

On the left hand, the Structure Point will buzz and otherwise feel pleasant when we are receiving impulses from our inner truth about structuring our environment. If we are resisting these impulses we will feel an expanding pain in the Structure Point, until we accommodate ourselves to new ways of doing things. If we are receiving pressure from our environment, such as someone trying to manipulate us, we will feel a constricting pain in the left Structure Point. Each person has the right to make their own decisions on how to structure their lives. When another person makes a decision about our behavior or timing without our permission, this becomes control or manipulation.

If we are taking action to schedule ourselves or restructure our environment in a beneficial way, we will feel pleasant buzzing sensations in the right hand Structure Point. If we feel constricting pain in this right hand point, it is a reminder either that we are trying to control someone else, or that we are squelching our own creative and spontaneous flow with too much structure.

I discovered the Structure Point while working with a client who had severe rheumatoid arthritis. As we began talking about her relationship with her mother, my client's outer left hand began to hurt very intensely near the wrist. She shared that her mother was very controlling towards her. Checking in with my inner guidance, I discovered that my client's pain was a warning about her mother's detrimental effect on her life through control.

As I began working with this body signal in my own life, I understood that it indicated both a need for positive change in my environment, and advice to "let go and let God," that is, to surrender my ego control over a situation.

Point 12: Spirit Guide Point. Point in the middle bottom of the palm, just above the wrist.

This point is an opening where our Guides can touch us directly when they want to get our attention. Each of us can make agreements with our Spirit Guides about how we wish to use this hand point. Our Guides can use the point to communicate with us as a unit (that is, as a group consciousness), or we can establish communication with one particular entity. One of our Guides could touch us on the right hand, and another on the left.

Buzzing on this hand point may be a springboard to validate the presence of our Guides. We may then choose to communicate with them through automatic or inspired writing, speaking, drawing or movement—various forms of what is known as channeling. They may also visit us in meditation. In Chapter 6 we will discuss techniques to deepen our communication with inner guidance.

Point 13: Unconditional Love Point. Mound of Venus, the rise on the palm just below the thumb.

Unconditional love is the feeling of love in the present moment, with no expectations for our own behavior or that of others in the future. This love vibration always involves merger with someone or something greater than our own ego; it is an emotional experience of the All. Buzzing on the Mound of Venus means that we are surrendering ourselves to the experience of unconditional love (left hand) or to channeling this energy to others (right hand).

Referring to the teachings of the philosopher Gurdjieff and of the spirit entity Michael, we may call the feeling of unconditional love an expression of the higher emotional center of consciousness. The lower emotional center connects us in personal relationships to other sentient beings. The higher emotional center connects us in relationship to the All. When we encounter people who are experiencing the higher emotional center, we may feel an energy field from them which emanates indiscriminate peace and love to their environment. As we surrender to this energy, we may feel a smile that takes over our face by itself, "for no reason," and that at the same time, the Mound of Venus is buzzing pleasantly on our hand.

Point 14: The Essence Point. Being truly yourself, acting from your core. The center of the palm of the hand.

Users of the Body Signals system feel the Essence Point vibrating when energy from their core is centering them. This point could be activated by a deep internal thought, a genuine emotional response or an impulsive action. It can validate that we are speaking our truth from the heart—what the Bible calls "witnessing." As we relax enough to let a message come through from the inner self, we may feel our Essence Point buzzing. A personal example: "I've always wanted to visit the sacred sites of England." The buzzing that I felt as I allowed this thought to surface, encouraged me to follow my heart and impulsively book the trip.

Point 15: The Acknowledgment Point. The middle of the inner wrist.

This point was discovered by my friend Darryl Schoenstadt as we were having dinner in a Milwaukee, Wisconsin restaurant.

The left inner wrist point indicates that we are receptive to the energy of appreciation and acknowledgment, whether it is directed toward us personally or is just "in the air." The Acknowledgment Point can help us read the coded, sometimes cryptic compliments that come from our loved ones when they are trying to be subtle in their praise. A pleasant buzzing in our left wrist will help us figure out that they are really saying, "Good job!" "I love you!" and other forms of appreciation coming from the heart. When we feel pain in the left wrist, it may indicate that we are having trouble receiving appreciation (expanding pain), or that we have merited acknowledgment which is not being given (constricting pain).

A constricting pain on the right wrist may indicate that we are projecting a negative thought of envy or jealousy to someone. ("You don't deserve thanks.") An expanding pain on the right wrist could indicate a grudging sort of acknowledgment where a more enthusiastic one is warranted. As we breathe into the pain and let our true feelings take over, it may become easier to give compliments without reservation—then the pain may become a pleasant sensation on out right wrist.

The Transpersonal Points

The transpersonal points on the hands and wrists relate to the interdimensional natures of our psyches, transcending time and space.

Point 16: Communication Point. The outer wrist just below the thumb.

When this point opened it was the first signal to appear on the back of the hand. Vibrations can occur here when a breakthrough or bonding occurs involving several people communicating with more than one dimension of consciousness (the group psyche of humanity, deeper levels of the unconscious, extraterrestrial sources of intelligence). Buzzing in the Communication Point signals to the participants that they are sharing a group energy for a particular project. Working with their soul consciousness, they are setting up a dynamic imagination structure for sharing ideas, creating their own morphogenic field, as it were (*cf.*, Sheldrake). This acts as a supportive grid of energy to help actualize the common project, which the participants will plug into as ideas, pictures and impulses to act spontaneously.

Vibrations on the Communication Point signal that the participants are exchanging energy in dynamic, open-ended ways. As they bounce around ideas and feelings, each one feels validated and encouraged to run with the energy in his or her own way. Each knows that he or she is a valuable part of the whole. Through linkage of the imaginations of the participants, a new common reality is formed. Acknowledgment of this dynamic energy structure leads to conscious, sustained cooperation. The meaning of the transpersonal Communication Point is distinct from the Relationship Point, which indicates an outer structured agreement with definite duties and promises; and from the Cooperation Point, which signals that energy is available for mutual benefit.

I remember feeling the Communication Point activated while sitting in meditation with a friend by the Santa Fe River in New Mexico. At the moment when the point started buzzing for both of us, my friend received the ability to plug into the Body Signals system at will. We each felt the energy of the system as part of a larger whole which had its basis in non-physical reality, although it reached its consciousness into the physical body. We were joined to a community of souls whose purpose was to communicate truth across the dimensions. Buzzing on the Communication Point was a validation of our inner connectedness to a larger Source.

Point 17: Alternate Reality Point. Back of the hand underneath the fold of skin between the thumb and forefinger (Cooperation Point).

This point is a window into the reality of our other incarnations and parallel lives. It differs from the Ring Finger Point in indicating an actual communication with the other incarnation, transcending time. The result may be a healing in so-called "past" time, or a transmission of helpful support into our present life, through the process of creating a mutually beneficial thought-form or energy structure.

Recently I facilitated a past life regression during which my client's Alternate Reality Point was buzzing strongly. She picked up information on two incarnations—the first was a lifetime in which she had used the Body Signals system in Old Kingdom Egypt for the purpose of sending healing energy through the hands. This memory was a very pleasant experience for my client. When she felt complete with that incarnation, her Alternate Reality Point began to buzz again very strongly. This time the alternate lifetime was a confused and angry person who needed her support and acknowledgment in order to move into the Light and find peace. In both instances the Alternate Reality Point signaled transformation for my client—the first, as she activated past life knowledge of the Body Signals system into her present body; the second, as she facilitated the transformation of her own patterns of confusion, by assisting her counterpart into the Light.

Point 18: Inner Child Point. The middle of the back of the hand, just below the middle finger.

This point has recently opened up for practitioners of Body Signals, as we incorporate more inner child work into our personal development. When the Inner Child Point is buzzing, it confirms that we are tuned into the unconscious aspects of Self, particularly our needs for safety and security. If we feel pain on this point, it could be a warning that the inner child's needs are being ignored or squelched by the rational mind or by distorted concepts of truth.

In Ho'oponopono, a version of a Hawaiian healing system taught by the late Morrnah Simeona, it is said that stroking the back of the hand is a good way to comfort the inner child. As we will discuss in the next chapter, the inner child is both a symbol of the unconscious mind and a gateway to its exploration. It acts as a bridge between our rational self and our soul consciousness.

Point 19: Compassion Point. Palm of hand, between Relationship and Essence points.

This point has recently activated as more practitioners are consciously **channeling** unconditional love through healing systems such as Reiki. It reminds us that our **essence** includes being in **relationship** to all sentient beings, as we embody Divinity in human form.

The above nineteen points represent the development of the Body Signals system in the hands thus far. I anticipate expansion and revision of this system over time: Body Signals is a living entity, with its own purpose for development.

Activating Your Personal Hand Code

My Spirit Guide Nathan says,

> *Intuition needs substantiation in everyday life. The Western culture does not validate knowledge coming from other dimensions of reality. So that you know that you know, it's important to have a few tactile sensations that capture your attention on a regular basis.*

In addition to the eighteen points listed in this book, some practitioners of Body Signals feel vibrations in specific parts of the fingers; or they may assign specific meanings to each part of a finger. For example, you might program the top joint of the forefinger (creativity) to indicate artistic expression, the middle joint to indicate prosperity and the lowest to indicate sexuality. You can program any part of your body to mean anything you want it to mean—or, more often, it will happen that you just know what the tingling in that part of your body means, without any conscious programming from your intellect.

—◄o►—

We conclude this chapter with a meditation to help activate some of your hand points. I suggest you tape record this meditation or have a friend talk you through it.

> *First*, lie down and breathe slowly and deeply. Imagine a grid of light floating in the air in front of you. Although this grid is complex, it has a welcoming feeling. You feel drawn to it. Breathe this grid into your body, slowly and deeply. You begin to feel several points on your skin vibrating and pulsing.

> *Now* you notice one point buzzing on one of your hands—is it the right or the left hand? This point on the hand is connected to a point on the grid of light. Breathe the grid of light into this point on your hand. Don't be concerned about the meaning of the hand signal point—just energize it with light.

Feel the grid of light pulsating, first in front of you, then within you, varying with each breath you take. First inhale the grid; then exhale—feel it in front of your body or above it. At some point you will feel a strong, unshakable connection between the hand point and the grid of light. It may be a tingling, a buzzing or a pulsation.

When you feel ready, let the grid of light go back to the space in front of you, knowing that you can call it back into your body at any time. Now stretch, yawn and open your eyes: You feel totally refreshed!

◄O►

I want to remind you that the Body Signals system is not "written in stone." Please feel free to experiment with it to find the signal points that work for you. I hesitated for some years to share this system publicly, not wanting to impose my personal truth on others. I knew that it is important for each person to develop his or her own truth. I encourage you to use this system of Body Signals as a springboard to enhance your sensitivity to your own inner truth.

Besides the signal points described in the previous two chapters, many other potential points exist. The present nineteen points have provided the basis and foundation of the system of spiritual sensitivity I have developed. Their purpose is to use the kinesthetic sense of the hands as a window to the wisdom of the Soul. The following chapters will describe how to tap into other parts of the body for the same purpose.

CHAPTER FOUR

◄〇►

Healing the Inner Child

In developing proficiency in using body signals, it is beneficial to clear up emotional blocks that keep us from accessing our unconscious mind in a clear way. Our bodies can develop ways of telling us when we are not communicating clearly with our unconscious, which I will also call the instinctual self. A symbol which evokes the unconscious mind is the inner child, the child within us. In this chapter we will explore the process of opening a relationship with the inner child through body signals—a relationship which can provide us with an emotional and physical foundation for developing our full potential.

There are several approaches to the inner child which can help us to center the psyche in inner truth and help it feel comfortable there. One important frame of reference involves finding our inner child in our physical body. As we learn to read our "gut feelings," that is, physical sensations in our solar plexus and stomach areas, we will find that our instinctual self will become more secure in its self-expression.

In several metaphysical traditions the solar plexus is considered one of seven energy centers in the body called *chakras* (wheels in Sanskrit). The solar plexus lies in the stomach area, just beneath the rib cage and above the navel. Esoteric tradition often connects this center with the individual's sense of identity, and with one's relationship to the outside world.

In the Kundalini system of energy circulation, originating in India and now widely practiced in the West, the solar plexus is known as the third chakra. Energy is said to ascend from the base of the spine to the top of the head, passing through the solar plexus before reaching the heart. Our perceptions of our outer reality (environment) reach directly into the solar plexus, and extend from it as cords of light. The interface between our beliefs and our perceptions determines the way we think of ourselves as individuals, both consciously and unconsciously.

Our beliefs and internal images about our identity and place in the world affect the security of our inner child, our instinctual self. One of the inner child's concerns is that the personality has a safe space where it can express itself. When our inner child's sense of security is shaky, our whole personality mechanism—the relationship between instinctual self, conscious mind and transcendent self—goes off-balance. The conscious mind will react to the outside world with mistrust, worry, pressure, defensiveness and aggression—behaviors that are out of touch with intuition and instinct, two forms of natural inner knowing. The transcendent self's attempts to communicate with the personality will be distorted and blocked by the fears of the inner child.

Fears and the Inner Child

In our society, the usual adult response to the fears of a child is to deny that any real threat to safety exists. The fears are said to be only imaginary. The child learns that he or she is supposed to be comforted by this denial of inner perception. The child is expected to surrender its fear to comfort or denial by the adult authority figure. However, a sense of disappointment may linger when the adult reassures,

"It's all right, honey," while the child still perceives intuitively or instinc-tively that things are not safe. If a three year old discerns that Uncle Henry has a black cloud around him, and so runs away when Uncle Henry tries to hug him, he is likely to be scolded for rude behavior. Being in touch with gut feelings, a child usually discerns safety or danger through sensations in the solar plexus or through seeing energy fields (auras) in the environment, rather than through adult logic.

Gradually, because of lack of validation of his/her psychic percep-tions from the parents and the school system, the child learns the "Ignore it and it'll go away" approach to fear and unpleasantness. Another variant is, "Pretend it's not there and it won't hurt you," like the proverbial ostrich with its head in the sand. As a result, often as adults we are out of touch with physical sensations which are meant to warn us of real physical or psychic danger. Tightness in the solar plexus can warn us of physical or psychic intrusion. In the same vein, sensations in the heart become activated when our emotional well-being is affected. On an intellectual level, we may respond with a head-ache when we are subject to mental coercion or pressure.

It is our system of beliefs, rather than some objective truth, that activates our body's response to pressure: In other words, perceived danger. This is why some people become paralyzed with fear in situa-tions which are harmless for others. One person may freeze up at the prospect of entering an elevator—his body literally will refuse to board! Someone else may take elevators for granted, and yet a third may find an elevator ride a pleasurable experience. The key to understanding our emotional responses can be found in our beliefs, which may or may not be mirrored in our outer experience of the moment. Often we find that we have accepted the validity of other people's experiences rather than our own, especially our parents' when we were children. If our sense of their authority over us has been strong enough, we will tend to dismiss our own sensory experiences if they do not conform to the beliefs of our authority figures.

The code of beliefs that we have adopted may be quite unconscious, so that even if it runs counter to everything we think we believe, we still act it out in our lives. If a parent has been irresponsible around the issue of debt, the child may adopt this pattern of behavior into his/her own life, even though the parent may have preached a value system of responsibility to the child at home. When the child grows up, he or she may recall the lectures: "My parents always taught me to be financially responsible," while repressing awful arguments and scenes around debt that went on in the home. The adult child will be very confused, denying that he or she is playing out the parental pattern around debt. "Where did I learn this behavior? Certainly not from my parents!"

I vividly remember taking on a pattern of parental fear at the age of three. My mother has a chronic and deep-seated fear of drowning. I don't know the origin of her phobia, but she has had it since childhood. I remember the moment when I adopted her fear as my reality—in that moment I became afraid of drowning in deep water. I was at the beach in Chicago with my parents. My father, who enjoyed swimming, thought that it was time I learned to swim too and decided on a direct approach, as usual. He had been holding me up; now he picked me up and started to toss me into Lake Michigan, which at that spot was about waist-deep for him.

At that point my mother yelled, "Don't you do that! Don't throw him in that water!" I remember a feeling like a heavy weight hitting me in the solar plexus as she screamed. At that moment I took on her fear of drowning. Although I now enjoy swimming, I am still leery of deep water. That day my mother's intense emotional fear for my safety won out over my father's pleasurable sense of ease and adventure in the water. My inner child adopted my mother's fears as truth, regardless of the objective facts of the situation.

As adults we learn to painstakingly let go of fears a little at a time—fears of our own making or from others—which have ruled our lives since childhood. In day to day living, we learn that it works to first acknowledge our fears and make them conscious before trying to dissolve them. We may feel that once we intellectually understand the falseness of a belief we can eliminate it quickly and live a life unencumbered by fear. However, the false belief will show up in our lives repeatedly so that we strengthen ourselves through the experience of healing and transforming it. Each time we send Light to our fears, we grow in a certain kind of strength that comes from deepening self-knowledge. As we move from feelings of anger and frustration to a sense of wholeness and peace, we reprogram our cells to accept the truth that WE ARE GOD and that we deserve love on all levels. Then we honestly can bless our fears and accept them as part of us, knowing that they are valuable signals for our interaction with the world.

The Three Selves

In the world view of the traditional Hawaiian culture, and in many other earth-centered cultures, the psyche is divided into three parts: Father (Transcendent Self, superconscious), Mother (conscious mind) and Child (Instinctual Self, unconscious mind). Traditional Freudian psychology has made a similar division. In earth-centered traditions a primary function of the conscious mind is to take care of the inner child. The inner child provides the link between Mother and Father, conscious mind and the transcendent self. The function of the transcendent self is to provide a gateway to the big picture of our soul's consciousness, so that our lives become suffused with meaning.

One of the most important aspects of this worldview is that the conscious mind, or ego, cannot grasp the soul's perspective without taking the unconscious mind (inner child) into account. Our inner child holds the memory bank of all the experiences we have ever had. It is thus well-equipped to read the layers of feeling which we experience in each life situation. These feelings must be acknowledged in all their complexity when we are communicating with transcendent self.

In the West, the patriarchal view of the last three thousand years has espoused a "grit your teeth" approach to life in which personal needs have been subordinated to a cause or power greater than the personal self. Feedback from the body has been pushed aside as unimportant or, indeed, as an obstacle to "getting on with it." The patriarchal emphasis on action at the expense of awareness has had dire consequences for our instinctual sensitivity. Through cultivation of our inner child sensations in the solar plexus we are able to find out how we are really feeling in the moment, instead of making commitments that we must break later. We are also able to tune into past traumas and feel what our inner child needs us to do to heal them.

By staying in the moment and paying attention to our present needs, we avoid the self-sabotage of forcing ourselves to do things we don't really want to do. A sales representative has scheduled a meeting with a potential client. He pushes himself to get the appropriate materials ready for the meeting, but becomes distracted every time he attempts to do so. He feels tired, with no energy to work on the project. Finally giving in to the flow, he focuses on a completely different work assignment, finding it most productive. Two hours before the scheduled meeting, the prospective client calls and cancels it. Since the sales representative has followed his instincts, he has not wasted time and energy on a meeting which, on a psychic level, he knew would not take place. His intuition has freed him up to use his available energy for more relevant projects.

In this situation the individual has successfully followed the same gut instinct that animals use before a storm, an earthquake or other natural disturbance. As animals we instinctively know probabilities—given what currently exists, our instincts can predict a likely outcome. Whether we call it the id, the subconscious, the inner child or the instinctual self, we must rehabilitate the gut level part of ourselves from the compost heap of fear to which Freud relegated it, mistrusting inner urges. As we trust that our inner child is actually our bridge to higher consciousness, we will create a grounded spirituality free from extremes of fanaticism and intolerance.

Ungrounded Spirituality

What happens when we don't listen to our inner child and force ourselves to do things we don't really want to do, or to make commitments we don't really want to make? We invite self-sabotage and eventually illness. We do not have fun with what we are doing, thus lowering our efficiency; or we drag our feet when it comes to implementing the commitment. I find that procrastination is often a good signal that I've committed to something I didn't really want in my life, or that now is not the proper timing for it.

When we force ourselves to implement the commands of a higher "God" outside ourselves, we can talk ourselves into many bizarre moral decisions. We have all read of mass murderers and cult leaders who claim that "God" or their "inner voice" told them to kill or to torture their victims. The soul's larger perspective is not the source of this so-called inner guidance.

An individual can completely cancel out the voice of the inner feelings, which may be screaming that the contemplated behavior is neither appropriate nor humane. If a person becomes enslaved to serving a vengeful and angry God, he or she may seek a kind of indirect power through "guidance" to do things which are "superhuman," that is, outside the basic moral law. One version of the moral law may be stated as follows: "As long as you cause no harm, do what you will." (Aleister Crowley)

Our inner child's needs for comfort and security act as a built-in check to prevent grandiosity, so that we cannot "play God" and make others' decisions for them. Instead we will spend time and attention taking care of our own inner needs. We see in the media the consequences of ignoring the needs of our own inner child and projecting its feelings of hurt and insecurity onto others: "God told me they had to be eliminated." "She was evil." "He was gay." "They were Catholics." "The Bible says that these people must be condemned." The list could go on. When violence happens in the name of God, an external moral code has taken precedence over the basic human ethic of the right to life. In harming another we are really harming ourselves, since separation is illusion. In denying another's right to exist we are also calling into question our own right to exist.

When we perpetrate violence in the name of a Higher Power, it is a signal that our basic survival instincts, the needs of our inner child, have not been respected and taken care of. In trying to take care of our abandoned child, we have played God within the confines of an oppressive belief system superimposed onto our personality, harming others as a result. In our search for security outside ourselves, our idea of "God's will" overrides both our common sense and our personal boundaries, so that we become perpetrators of the pain of others. In the service of an angry God, our inner child can turn mean and ugly. If it has been taught that selfishness is wise and mature, it may try to grab whatever pleasure is available "before it's too late."

At this time in our society we see a great deal of inner desperation, where the inner children of many adults strike out blindly in destructive or compulsive behavior. Not really believing that their true needs will be met, people try to plug up their inner feelings of emptiness with addictions. It seems that many souls have incarnated now who have carried inner child wounds for lifetimes. Many of us have been born with this issue. We create opportunities to work out issues of addiction, replacing it with balance. This means respecting the needs of our inner child above all other perceived needs. If we use basic morality, we will fulfill our responsibilities to our children and to others with whom we have commitments. However, we will not use our commitments as an excuse to renege on our inner parenting. By parenting ourselves we will see to it that we live free of addiction in all its forms. Each day will bring us more in touch with our personal instincts as we actually live according to our gut feelings.

Because of the importance of relating consciously to the inner child, this chapter occurs earlier than the ones on inner guidance. Practitioners of the Body Signals system have found that inner guidance can be reliable only when the personality is secure in taking care of personal needs. They have learned to pay careful attention to the feelings in the solar plexus, particularly on the left side, while making decisions.

The left side of the abdomen, according to the above-mentioned healer Morrnah Simeona, is the seat of the inner child. In some Native American traditions (e.g. the Mayan) a woman is said to have a hole on the left side of the abdomen after giving birth. In doing physically-oriented inner child work we plug up that hole in the abdomen with love and concern.

The Safe Space Technique

The purpose of this meditation is to get you in touch with your inner child. You may want to have a friend talk you through this, or to dictate the material into a tape recorder and play it back while meditating.

First, assume a comfortable position. Place your hands on your solar plexus, just above the navel, off to the left a little. Take several deep breaths. (Pause.) Now use your imagination and create a stillpoint, a sanctuary, a safe place for your inner child. This can be a garden, a park, woods, a beach, meadow or field—anywhere that your inner child feels comfortable. Continue to breathe slowly and deeply. Imagine yourself there in your safe space with your inner child. This place belongs to him or her—no one besides you can be there, unless your inner child gives them permission to enter.

Allow your imagination to picture your inner child vividly—accept you first impressions of his or her age, clothing and mood. Does your inner child seem happy, or sad? Quiet, or extroverted? Breathe deeply and allow your inner child to become real for you. Through this breath you are establishing permanent contact. If it feels appropriate, go over and touch your inner child; perhaps give a hug, or hold hands. Breathe deeply and relax. Now ask your inner child to show you something in the safe space which sparks his or her interest.

Trust your first impressions. Allow yourself to share in your inner child's interest or enthusiasm. Continue to breathe in slowly and deeply, relaxing as you exhale. Now ask your inner child for a suggestion to have fun. You might ask, "What can the two of us do today, in the outside world, to have fun together?" Receive and consider your inner child's suggestion. If you feel it's not practical, negotiate—find out what you could feasibly do together that would be fun. Take into account what your inner child really wants to do—tretch your adult reasoning a little. Then make an agreement to DO IT!

Continue to breathe deeply, safe with your inner child in your safe space.

At this point it would be good to make an agreement with your inner child that you will do at least **one fun thing every day** with him or her, no matter what. Feel the joy of this commitment. Keep breathing deeply. (Pause.) When you feel complete, thank your inner child, your basic inner self, for being there with you. Promise to visit him or her in your safe space often, every day if possible. When you feel ready to return to the outer adult world, count to three, squeeze your thumbs and...you're back! Shake out your hands and feet and then stretch.

The Safe Space Technique can give you easy access to the inner child and its wisdom. At some point you may want to ask your inner child if he or she would like to bring a friend into the safe space you have created together. It could be your higher self, a friendly power animal, a Spirit Guide, or a trusted loved one or friend. Remember—no coercion! Respect the pace and timing of your inner child, as well as its desire to reconnect and just spend time with you, without an agenda.

The Guides' Message for the Inner Child

From my Guide Betty, who works with self-acceptance:

> *This part of you, your inner child, is to be cajoled, catered to, stroked. This establishes a healthy relationship with those parts of you that realize that you are here for yourself, for your own growth, and not for the convenience of the society you live in. If everyone is living out of their inner child, there will be conflict— no doubt about it. Living from the inner child space will not bring peace, but it will bring a lot more creative expression on your planet. This is most important at this time—to bring creative solutions to bear on your issues, to experiment with creating on a local level. Once the new structures are in place—they will be changed! This is not the time for a new dogma to replace your outmoded beliefs. You all, as a species, will learn to live without*

dogma, with only your inner knowing to guide you. Your fron-
tiers have shifted so fast, in terms of your technologies and your
consciousness of the needs of the world that the global mind
brings. Now your spiritual emphasis is how to shift focus con-
tinuously, keeping pace without losing your center.

I am here to tell you that you have just begun the process of your
evolution toward the goal of heaven on earth that so many of you
espouse. The first step is a shift in your own consciousness; the
second is group action. Both are important, and will come at dif-
ferent stages. You are already involved in the transformation of
your planet, and will continue to be. You cannot halt this pro-
cess now. Any cooperative energy on your part will be greeted
with great enthusiasm from the Gardeners of the Earth—those
Spirits who have traveled great distances through time to be here
for your transformation. Any resistance you may have will be
lovingly caressed until such time as you are ready to let go of it.

We know that the goal of your planet's transformation consists
in the reflowering of talent as a responsibility to the species. That
is, you fulfill your responsibility to the species that raised you
by letting your talent flower for the greater good of all. This does
not mean that you should uphold cultural norms that you no
longer agree with; rather, we encourage you to use your ingenu-
ity to create new forms for needed human experiences: Birth, ini-
tiation, marriage, childraising, death and others. Each person has
the right to be recognized for who he or she is, no matter what
the circumstances. This is primary. When this recognition
becomes a fundamental priority, your society will be healed.

Decision-Making And Gut Feelings

When the safety signals of the solar plexus are ignored, we may get
our inner child into uncomfortable situations. We may make
commitments we can't keep, or plans that are not feasible. Often it is
difficult to extricate ourselves gracefully from these situations.

A hypothetical example: A desperate friend calls, needing to see you right now. You feel a queasiness in your stomach—you already have a long-awaited dinner engagement with other friends. Nevertheless you say, "Come on over." You phone your other friends and cancel your plans with them. Your needy friend arrives and takes up several hours of your time, wallowing in self-pity. When the episode is finally over you feel drained and exhausted, wondering why you didn't follow your gut feeling earlier, and just say no. As you tune into your inner child space you find a frightened and angry being there, who cries, "Why don't you ever pay attention to ME?"

The lesson here is not to never change your plans, but rather to recognize the importance of the solar-plexus as a guide in decision-making. If a plan feels good on the left side of your gut, do it. If it doesn't feel good, don't do it.

Another pitfall is to assume the role of an adult who tries to comfort the child (inner or outer) by first denying that danger exists, and then by placating the fearful child by giving candy, toys and other substitutes for the fear. This is really an attempt to plug up the energetic hole in the child's solar plexus (or in the adult's) even as the adult denies that there are any valid grounds for fear. As adults, we may suffer from a food, alcohol or drug addiction, as a way of filling up the void that we feel when security issues (for example, abandonment) come up in our lives.

Since working with John Bradshaw's seminars I have found that the right side of the solar plexus mirrors the fears or desires of others with whom we are linked psychically. It has been a great relief to acknowledge that many of the fears I was feeling were not mine at all! I had been carrying them for my loved ones. Now my priority and that of my students is to shed other people's burdens so that we can pay more attention to our own inner child and satisfy its needs. When we try to live by other people's fears and policies, the right side of the abdomen warns us through pain.

Instead of pouring oil on the waters to calm (suppress) our fears, we can breathe love into the tight, constricting feelings in the solar plexus as they come up. We can ask, "What issues are you reflecting in my life? The response may be immediate or subtle—perhaps by randomly opening an inspirational book or through the chance remark of a friend. When we truly feel grateful for all the signals our body gives us, whether they are pleasant or not, we are well on our way to integrating (becoming whole with) our addictions. If we feel compelled to eat a box of cookies, we can tune into our stomach and see how it will feel after the box is consumed. Based on past experience, our body can indicate how we are likely to feel after a given course of action.

My personal experience with my "bloody nose signal" (See Chapter 9) has pivoted around the issue of denial of my true feelings. This stems from programming from childhood: "You mustn't feel that way—that's not nice!" "Don't bother to want that—you can't have it." I remember being placated as a child so that I wouldn't make too many demands and cause trouble. My father's drinking and gambling addictions were a major drain on the family resources, so I learned to keep my desires small. Even though my adult experience is that I can ingeniously find ways to do what I want, the old tape of self-denial will creep in sometimes with its message, "You're not worthy!" Perhaps my bloody noses are an instantaneous form of grief about denying my wishes, a form of the tears I find so hard to shed as an adult male.

Trusting Gut Feelings

The inner child is a symbol for our basic survival instincts. We may be afraid that if we give in to these instincts, our lives will be chaotic and undisciplined. We may have been taught as children to repress our desires automatically, and so now mistrust our basic instincts. However, by working with our inner child consistently, not as a hurt memory of the past, but as a living, essential part of us in the NOW, we will soon progress to a deeper understanding of our real needs. Soon our inner child will go beyond the "I *want some ice cream!*" stage, to voice what really makes us happy and fulfilled on an essence level.

It is good to pay attention to both sides of the solar plexus consistently, right and left. The left side acts as an indicator of our own gut instincts about a situation, the right as a signal for the programming we carry from others. As we get in the habit of acting on our own gut instincts we will observe improvement in the level of our self-trust.

The Yes and No System

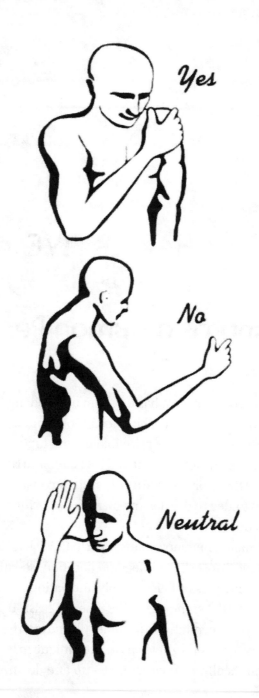

CHAPTER FIVE

Working as a Human Pendulum

Many years ago I learned a basic system of receiving "yes" and "no" answers to questions put to the unconscious mind. Within this system practitioners used the principle of moving the spine to get a response—back and forth, right and left; similar to the concept of the pendulum. After working with this system consistently for several years, I was guided to develop my own way of using the body to contact the unconscious.

It came about one snowy afternoon in Chicago. A friend was leading an "Essene" workshop on food preparation, so-called because he based it on principles of living simply and eating raw foods, as practiced by the Jewish Essene sect at the time of Christ. Toward the end of the workshop we meditated to become still and feel the subtle motions of our bodies. My friend guided us in a technique to let our right arms move automatically, as they wished—up and down, away from the body and toward it. All we had to do, my friend said, was to relax deeply enough, and the arm would move of its own accord, effortlessly.

During the meditation I felt my body surrounded by a vast grid of energy lines. As I plugged into one line of energy my arm would move by itself. I felt propelled into a level of trance where my reality seemed unbounded by time or space: A kind of creative reverie in which many ideas could gel. At some point during this meditation I realized that the technique could be adapted to get "yes" and "no" answers from my unconscious. Soon after this workshop I was using my right arm routinely for this purpose. Over the years the technique has expanded to include "neutral" or "no opinion" answers as well.

The following procedure may be helpful in programming your arm to act as a pendulum, as illustrated in the accompanying pictures:

1) *Move* your right arm (or left, if you are left-handed) back and forth, toward your trunk and away from it, at chest or throat level. Your arm should be crooked slightly at the elbow—relaxed, not rigid.

2) *Breathe* deeply. Relax into a motion of least resistance. You will feel a pathway of energy where your arm movement is effortless, toward the chest and away from it. Usually this pathway will be a line of energy from the middle of the chest to beyond the right shoulder.

3) *When you feel* comfortable with this back and forth motion, crook your arm and move it up to touch your right shoulder (if you are using the right arm); then move it down to waist level, extending forward. You will find another pathway of effortlessness as the hand moves up to touch the shoulder and returns to a forward position.

Practice this movement awhile.

4) ***When you feel*** comfortable with these two energetic pathways of arm movement, you are ready
to ask questions of your unconscious mind. The
answer code is as follows: Movement of the arm
toward your trunk indicates a "yes" answer;
movement away from your torso indicates a "no"
answer; and arm movement up and down in front
of the shoulder indicates a "no opinion" or "neutral" answer.

5) ***Begin*** your practice by getting yourself into a
relaxed state and asking simple questions, especially those you are emotionally neutral about.
"Will it snow somewhere in Alaska today?" (Probably yes.) "Have I known my friend _____
in a previous life?" (Be careful to breathe deeply
and stay relaxed with this one.) "Would home
repairs be a good project to undertake this year?"
Take note of the answers that come, while feeling
the sensations of flowing with the path of least resistance through your arm movements.

6) ***Continue*** to practice the arm movements each
day. You will notice that, depending on the type
of question, your arm may be drawn to different
parts of your body: Throat, third eye, solar plexus,
to name a few.

Clarity in "Yes" and "No" Questioning

To use this technique successfully, two factors must be considered. One
is relaxation; it is important to approach the unconscious mind in a
relaxed way. Deep, slow, consistent breathing helps, as does visualizing the arm moving without effort, before physically doing the

technique. Some people find that visualizing certain colors, such as indigo blue, helps them relax deeply enough to enter the so-called Alpha state, a realm of consciousness where answers from the non-physical portions of self are readily available to the conscious mind.

The second factor, which is related to relaxation, is emotional detachment from the issue asked about. We must let go of mental pressure about the outcome, not trying to control the answer the subconscious mind gives to us, but giving it the space to provide an answer from our own inner truth. This can require a great deal of inner discipline. If we have been playing the lottery for weeks on end, it may be tempting to ask the question, "Will I win big in the lottery this week?" and then force our arm in a movement toward the chest, indicating a "yes" answer. If the win does not happen that week, we will be disappointed, inclined to blame our unconscious for not knowing the truth. Or we may blame the technique itself for being deficient and give up using it. Instead, it would be good to examine our frame of mind while asking the question. Are we tense, nervous? Are our body movements relaxed? Do we really feel a part of a larger energy grid? Do we have an attitude of "divine detachment" which holds that no matter what the outcome, our life will continue to progress as it should?

It's ironic—first we must phrase our mental question clearly and directly. Then we must stand out of the way, taking a breath and saying, in effect, "This, or something better, Universe." The moment of our surrender provides the universe with the opening it needs to move our desires into physical reality. "A watched kettle never boils."

I had an experience of this surrender while experimenting with dice. I tried to get the pattern "1, 6" to come up consistently, using one die. To be successful, I found I had to look away from the die as I threw it. Looking away gave the universe a chance to manifest the pattern I wanted. If the pattern was interrupted (for example 1, 4), I had to start over at the beginning and throw for a "1," not a "6."

Practitioners of this technique often receive their clearest answers with "one hand not knowing what the other is doing." They will be thinking about one issue when suddenly, "out of nowhere," an answer about a completely different issue will come to mind, clearly and forcefully. Perhaps they had been pondering that issue and had put it aside. Or perhaps just being in a deeply relaxed state provides the unconscious mind with the access it needs to feed us information.

The Workings of the Human Pendulum

Because my personal train of thought is more often in the form of words than pictures, my arm will sometimes move spontaneously in response to unspoken ideas I have formed in my head. People who are more highly visual may respond to inner pictures more easily. Those who have developed their kinesthetic sense (processing information by gut feeling) may find that when a certain feeling comes over them, their arm moves spontaneously to confirm or deny that feeling. Or one may be browsing in a bookstore when his hand spontaneously reaches for a book, then gives him a "yes" answer by moving toward his chest. All this may seem to occur without the participation of the conscious mind—body wisdom predominates in all of our lives from time to time, whether we are primarily kinesthetic or not.

Many people use objects such as paper clips, crystals, coins, etc. to act as pendulums and are successful at tapping their unconscious with these tools. I initially learned to use my spine as a pendulum, and so have always felt more comfortable with body-pendulum techniques. In the context of Body Signals, I feel it is good practice to use the arm or spine as a pendulum, to allow the cells of the body access to the universal life energy as often as possible. This way the body becomes accustomed to experiencing deeper levels of truth. This helps the body to break up patterns which have become detrimental to physical and emotional health, restoring itself to smooth functioning through the natural healing process. The practice of using the arm as a pendulum also illustrates that there is no real separation between the spiritual and the physical—the seeming barriers come from our own minds.

The "Michael" material (previously mentioned in Chapters 3 and 4), in common with many other philosophical systems, holds that the subconscious mind contains memories of our experiences from the beginning of our creation (the casting of the soul from the Tao, or

Source). Our psyche contains higher centers of consciousness through which we can access the truth our souls have put together as a result of our experiences. In our culture these higher centers have usually been accessed only at times of great stress or epiphany (awakening). Developing the kind of sensitivity in the body that Body Signals promotes will gain us increased access to these higher centers, where experiences of great strength, universal understanding and unconditional love can occur.

Through the experience of physicalized intuition the body naturally acts a bridge between the higher and lower centers, helping universal wisdom to become grounded in physical terms. We might say that our five bodies—physical, etheric, emotional, mental and spiritual—are the repositories of all the wisdom we have gathered through time. We even have cellular access to wisdom we have learned outside of time! As we allow our bodies to be conscious conduits for signals from the soul, we will never feel alone. We will no longer be trapped behind the barricades of our belief systems. Instead, we will feel that we are connected to the Source of our own truth.

Healing Emotional Blocks

One may tap into several frequencies of "extrasensory" information through asking "yes" and "no" questions. One level of information might be labeled the data bank of collected experiences known as the subconscious mind. Another might be called the integrated wisdom of the soul's perspective—the higher self or superconscious. It is important to draw a distinction between the realm of the subconscious (base self, inner child—see Chapter 4) and the soul's perspective because, in addition to supportive instincts and memories, the subconscious also contains unresolved conflict and trauma.

We may need emotional cleansing and healing in a specific area of life—relationships, for example. If we have a block in that area, we may not be able to achieve the emotional detachment necessary to get clear and consistent answers from our subconscious when we ask about relationships. Whether we feel clear or not, it is nonetheless beneficial to ask the inner child what he or she is feeling about a current situation, so that we consciously recognize where the blockages are in our psyche. If we are detached enough to ask both our higher self and our inner child for their input into a situation, we will open ourselves to a broader, more comprehensive version of our personal truth. Our higher self will give us an overview, while our inner child will reflect our current emotional reality, blockages and all.

Ultimately the most important thing is to respect where the inner child is at in this moment in the decision-making process, so that we do not push ourselves to make enlightened decisions before healing the relevant block, thus suppressing our current feelings, irrational though they may seem. An individual may have a general policy of maintaining an "open relationship" with his or her partner. Yet if the partner announces that he or she is involved emotionally or sexually with someone else, the individual's first reaction may be one of rage, followed by depression as overwhelming abandonment feelings come up. Rather than swallowing these feelings and forcing oneself to look at the situation from the partner's perspective, it may be healthier for the individual to focus attention on comforting the inner child. When the inner child feels loved and reassured by the conscious mind, then the individual can be honestly open to guidance from the higher self, spirit friends and loved ones.

Communicating with Other Life Forms

When we have achieved the detachment necessary to get clear answers from the non-physical portions of our personal reality—the inner child, the higher self and our Spirit Guides—we can experiment with asking questions of various consciousnesses outside ourselves. I subscribe to the traditional Hawaiian belief, common in earth-centered cultures, that everything has three aspects to self—the base self (the inner child; called in Hawaiian *unihipili*), the conscious mind (*uhane*) and the higher self or soul connection (*aumakua*). The basic self of so-called inanimate objects carry the vibrations of their past experiences, just as the higher self of a table is aware of its part in the grand scheme of things. With detachment, we can tune into the different selves of the animals, plants, crystals and inanimate objects in our environment, asking them questions and thus feeling connected to the broader purpose of things in a tangible way. We could ask the dining room table, "Would you like a vase of flowers at this time?" "Do you like this tablecloth?"

Asking "yes" and "no" questions of the basic selves of the beings and objects in my environment has been a refreshing and humbling experience for me. I am learning to follow their responses. Recently my car indicated that it wanted to go into the garage on a certain day. Since that day wasn't convenient, I persuaded my car (I thought) to let me take it in one day later. At the end of the originally suggested day my car's timing belt stopped working(!) and it had to be towed into my garage!

In October 1989 I was driving from Mt. Shasta to the San Francisco Bay area. Tuning into my timing for my journey that day, I heard the inner voice say, *"Be there by 5 o'clock."* I was puzzled at the strong force of the message, but obeyed it and pulled into my destination at 4:30. At 5:04 P.M. the 8.1 earthquake occurred—at the place where I was, there was no damage.

I find that asking questions of the environment is a good way to break our modern alienation from our surroundings. Just as we can become more sensitive to the physical environment through the physical pendulum technique, we can also open up to non-physical sources of information, including those thought of as extra-terrestrial. As we recognize that separation is illusion, that we are connected to all beings, we will be able to attract non-human intelligences who also come from feelings of unity and love. It's the universal law, "Like attracts like."

We might want to start our communication with non-human intelligences by asking questions of our earth brethren, the cetaceans (porpoises, dolphins and whales). Then we might expand our communication to so-called less evolved physical species. After we become accustomed to receiving direct communication from other physical species, the leap to non-physical intelligences will not seem as mind-boggling. We may find that it's not as hard to make contact as we had thought.

According to those who have successfully channeled cetacean energy, the most important factor is communicating with an open heart, rather than with abstract reasoning. Dolphins and whales do not use abstract reasoning in the same way that we do and do not understand theoretical questions. However, their sense of inter-connectedness with each other and with other life forms is much more highly developed than ours—they know they are part of the Whole, and live accordingly. We can learn this sense of unity from them. As long as we are communicating with true feeling, we will be under-stood. Emotions of oneness propel the drive for communication between our species and the cetaceans.

Technique for Communication

Let's take this opportunity to experience the body pendulum technique in a meditation designed to open up receptivity to other forms of con-sciousness. Do this technique now, or whenever you are so inclined. If you don't feel like doing it now, save it for later!

I recommend that you create a calm, peaceful environment for this meditation, a place where a friend can talk you through it with-out interruption, or where you can listen to your own voice on tape. If at any time during this exercise you wish to return to usual waking consciousness, all you have to do is put your thumbs into the palms of your hands and squeeze them with your fingers. In a moment you'll be back in your body in familiar surroundings.

One of the purposes of this exercise is to experience unconditional love. During the meditation, program yourself to be aware of the Mound of Venus Point underneath your thumb—the body signal point for unconditional love, or higher emotional center.

First, lie down and allow yourself to relax. Take several slow, deep breaths. As you breathe, you will gradually feel your-self sinking first into the floor, then into the earth.

Next, gently move your pendulum arm toward your chest and then away from your body. Do this a few times. Then move your hand first toward your shoulder, then away from it. Remember that in this system, arm movement toward the trunk of the body means "yes." Arm movement away from the body means "no." Movement toward the shoulder is a neutral answer.

Now, deeply inhale a soft purple light. Breathe it into every cell of your body. Tell your body that you want to relax down to a very deep level. As you continue to breathe deeply you will feel all your tension drain out through the floor, into the earth and out the other side into the cosmos.

At this time, call on the benevolence and love of your Soul and of your Spirit Guides, or call on your Higher Power as you understand it. Ask your Higher Power to guide you now, to help you experience a consciousness that is friendly and will foster your spiritual growth. Breathe deeply as we count to three—*one, two, three...*

Now you are in a place where you can ask questions of another form of consciousness. It could be a dolphin, a tree, a favorite animal, a crystal or someone who lives on another planet. Call this form of consciousness *FRIEND.* When you are ready to communicate with your *FRIEND,* you will feel a buzzing at the bottom of your hand where it meets your wrist—the Spirit Guide Point. Breathe deeply in a relaxed way and let your hand move toward you and away from you.

Now, if you are so inclined, give permission for *FRIEND* to move your arm gently while giving you "yes" and "no" answers. Start by asking some simple questions; you might ask, "*FRIEND*, do you have a message for me?" "Have we known each other in another existence?" "On this planet? On another planet?"

When you feel comfortable with *FRIEND*'s energy you might evolve to other questions requiring more than a "yes" or "no" response. "What is the purpose of our communication?" You might also ask, "After this meditation, would you like to guide me in making a visual drawing of your form? Would you like to write through me, to put our shared experience into words?" "Would it be appropriate for you to move your energy through my body so that I can feel you more fully?"

When you have communicated clearly with the energy pattern of your new *FRIEND* using words, pictures or feelings, thank this entity for coming to this dimension to visit with you. Make plans to meet again when it feels right to both you and *FRIEND.*

To come out of the meditation, take several deep breaths, filling yourself with a soft pink light. Then squeeze your thumbs in your palms and...**you're back!** Slowly get up and stretch, refocusing your attention on your physical environment.

Upon returning, you may want to make notes or drawings of your experiences. You can tap into *FRIEND*'s reality anytime you want, through your intention—it's just a matter of relaxing into the right energy grid.

Subtleties of Using the Energy Grid

Users of this "yes" and "no" system find that their arm moves automatically toward different parts of the body, depending on how the question posed relates to their life. For a long time after I started using this system, my right arm would always move toward the middle of my chest when giving me a "yes" answer. Traditionally in esoteric study, the heart or thymus chakra (energy center) is located in the middle of the chest, not exactly at the organ of the heart. I felt my arm movement as a signal from my unconscious mind that I was connecting to my heart wisdom, the truth of my essence.

More recently my arm often moves toward my throat, especially when I am asking questions relating to communication and relationships. When this happens I am aware of tapping into a distinct energy grid to receive answers from the unconscious. This helps me to understand that each energy grid contains the information which is specific to its own band of frequencies. One's arm may move to the root chakra (pelvic area), the third eye (forehead) or to the solar plexus, depending on the nature of the information sought. The root center would be activated by questions concerning physical creativity, sexual and otherwise, including meeting one's personal survival needs. The third eye center (ajna chakra) is related to mental creativity and telepathic communication; it is traditionally associated with the practice of Magic, that is, conscious co-creation of one's own reality. The solar plexus center beneath the rib cage would give information relating to personal boundaries as well as psychic linkages with one's loved ones, business associates and environment.

It is not always important to know in advance where your hand will travel when you ask a question. It is necessary to have enough detachment so that you will not try to control your hand as it moves from center to another.

Limitations of "Yes" and No" Questioning

A common question I hear from students is, "Are there any limitations to the kinds of questions I can ask when I use the 'yes' and 'no' system?" Almost any type of question can be posed, as long as you are not surrendering your personal power to something "outside" yourself. To put it another way, it's important not to separate yourself from your power by externalizing it—thinking that the truth, the wisdom, the abundance, the good judgment is "out there" rather than inside yourself. If you externalize your power sources, you may become dependent on specific techniques or people to make your decisions. Pendulums, astrology, tarot cards, the I Ching—all can take on a mystifying aura, instead of being recognized as an extension of your own consciousness. One advantage of using your body as a magical tool is that it may be harder to pretend that the power lies outside of you!

A good attitude toward systems of divination is that they can give you additional information relevant to the issue at hand, but should not short circuit your decision-making process. Usually you will know instinctively when the time is right to ask your unconscious mind for additional information. Sometimes it is better to gather external data and puzzle things out for yourself for awhile. If you feel a constriction or a tightness in your body as you ask a question, you might consider putting aside the interrogation process and just going with your flow.

In our first years of checking things out with Spirit Guides, it is usual to ask them about everything from major life issues to what color shirt to wear that day. After I had done this to my Guides for several years, one day I received the message, "Stop asking such trivial questions! You know the answers to these things—we refuse to be placed on a pedestal any longer!" My Guides made it very clear that they were my friends, but that it was not their job to make my decisions for me.

One of the most common instances of giving one's power away lies in not taking the time to ask, "What do I really want in this situation?" Our Guides cannot tell us what we should feel or what our goal should be. Certainly our inner child, symbol of our unconscious, will have input for us if it feels we will really listen. The "yes" and "no" system is one of the most effective ways to get in touch with our inner child, gently prodding it to make its needs and desires known. Our higher mind can point out additional information, such as how our life purpose could be furthered by acting on a particular opportunity, or by releasing a certain situation. But because of the principle of free will, it is rare for so-called higher consciousness to take over our decision-making process without permission from our inner child, our personal survival instincts.

My higher self (soul consciousness) says, "It is our function more to provide data and to remind people of their true purpose in life than to make their decisions for them." It is likely that our next decision will best be made by the conscious mind in combination with the other aspects of Self, not superseded by them. It is our responsibility to find out what our real values are, what really motivates us and to base our decisions on that inner knowing. The "yes" and "no" system is not meant to be a substitute for self-knowledge, but rather an enhancement tool.

Predicting the Future

According to the Spirit Guide Seth, as channeled by the late Jane Roberts (*cf. Seth Speaks*), certain lines of development, called probabilities, are likely to happen based on decisions which we and others make now and have made previously. If through our choices we veer onto another course, another line of development, the original probability will not manifest in this physical reality. Seth maintains however that each potential line of development will manifest in some version of reality, even if it's not the one we are consciously inhabiting now. We can also shift from one probability to another, depending on our choices of the moment. ("Should I meet my friends at the club as planned? What do I really want to do?") Each decision we make may change the course of our life, either to diverge from our original line of development or to get us back on our original track.

Some probabilities are stronger than others, based on the soul's urge for essence expression. Usually the soul does not care so much about the particular form of manifestation as much as the experience of the self within that situation. For example, we usually pick our marriage partners (either in this lifetime or before it) based on a probable set of lessons to be learned, not so much because we must be with a particular partner, no matter what.

When we ask our arm to give us a response to a question, such as, "Will I make a million dollars in the stock market this year?", the accuracy of the answer is contingent not only upon our current emotional detachment, but also upon the decisions we make during the year in question. I believe that neither the higher self nor any other level of consciousness can predict the future with unfailing accuracy, because of the dynamics of choice involved along the path from idea to manifestation. It might be better to phrase a financial question like this, "Higher self, does investment in _____ increase my chances for earning my desired profit this year?" Then let your arm move in the direction of "yes," "no" or "neutral."

Notice that the inner self responds to the intent behind the question; it does not play games with semantics. If you try to force your arm to give you the answer you want, you will not get accurate information. If you want to explore intimacy with a new partner, you might ask, "Is it in my best interest to get to know this person better?" Let's say your arm responds positively. You ask, "Would it be a good idea to have dinner together on Saturday?" and your arm responds "no." Disappointed, but detached, you ask, "What about Friday?" and you get a "yes." You call your friend and find out that he or she has other plans for Saturday night, but for some reason is free Friday. Your detachment has paid off!

Integrating "Yes" and "No" Into Daily Life

The "yes" and "no" system can provide us with input from both our subconscious mind (inner child) and superconscious mind (higher self), as well as from our discarnate friends and the "inner child" of everything around us. This system seems to work best when it is used to validate already existing impulses or to provide data needed to make a clear decision.

Implementing a "yes" and "no" system in the way it works best for each of us, whether through the arm motions described, or finger motions, muscle testing, a pendulum, or "heads-tails" of a coin, can be a useful tool to expand the limits of the conscious mind and, yes, to know the probable future. Most important, it can help us to know our beliefs and our blocks to physical and auric wholeness. It can become a tool that we use automatically to gain greater insight into all our affairs. When we're walking or driving down the street and a thought comes to mind, we can check it out with "yes-no."

With practice our arm or hand motion will become quite subtle so that only those who work with energy fields will be able to tell that we are "checking things out." We can use the technique at business meetings in conjunction with the hand signals paradigm. We might ask, "Do I have all the information I need to make a responsible decision?" Then our little finger buzzes as our forefinger moves slightly towards our chest. A double "yes!" "Inner child, do you support me working late tonight?" "Spirit Guides, do you have any suggestions for me to enhance my creativity...prosperity...love life?" Then we can pause to record the suggestions that come through while we are in a place of centeredness. When we receive unexpected "no" answers, we may wish to rethink our priorities. If we feel blocked when we try to receive information in this way, it may help to just relax, follow our immediate impulses and enjoy life.

This chapter concludes with a brief message from my Spirit Guide Li, the philosopher:

> *Using the "yes" and "no" technique puts you more firmly in your body while you are "tuned into" different levels of consciousness. You therefore do not neglect the body while you are expanding your capacity to apprehend truth in ever-growing ways. Your body participates in your expansion of consciousness, and is grateful. Not the least benefit of this technique is that you must get to a deep level of relaxation for it to work. This ensures that your body is nourished by the Universal Life Force on a frequent basis.*

CHAPTER SIX

◀〇▶

Working with Spirit Guides

Some people personify the source of inner guidance—for example, I have angels named Betty and Nathan. Others call their guidance the still small voice, the inner self or Holy Spirit. My students and I work with several aspects of spiritual guidance—the Source (Holy Spirit level), the Oversoul, which includes all the soul's lifetimes and the upper astral level which Spirit Guides inhabit. We also work with the world teachers who have descended to earth (the Infinite Souls of the Michael system)—Christ, Buddha, Lao-Tsu and Krishna. We may contact any soul who is "in the Light" (one with Source) and open to give guidance.

In my work I make a distinction between Spirit Guides and the higher self—Spirit Guides are our friends in the Light who are in between bodies or have graduated the physical plane, while our higher self represents our own soul's wisdom as it can be communicated to us. The inner aspects of self—the inner child, the higher self—are the foundation of our communication with our inner truth, which comes from the Oversoul. Our Oversoul has unlimited access to all the information we need to fulfill our life's purpose.

Because the physical plane is a plane of personalities, many of us feel reassured by the personal aspects of Spirit. These entities are intimately connected with our Oversoul and its perspective. We can call them Spirit Guides, messengers of God or our Guardian Angels. Usually they are beings who have lived on earth and are either "in between lives" or have graduated the earth plane and no longer need to be physical. Their purpose in their work with us is to help us see our life from our soul's perspective—from the big picture standpoint. They can help us with questions such as, "Will this action support my overall development?" "Is there something important that I'm not looking at in this situation?" "In your opinion, is it wise to make a choice in this situation at this time?"

In my twenty-plus years of experience with my Guides, and in the experience of many of my friends and students, we have found that our Guides are often our friends from other lifetimes. Often we have been involved together in intimate relationships such as parent/child, lovers, comrades-in-arms and employer/employee. These spirits are acting as our Guides because of a strong love bond. The Guide role helps them to integrate lessons they worked on when they were on earth. As a result of their relationship with us, they may make the decision to return to earth in physical bodies and to re-experience these lessons from a new perspective. One example might be a Guide who assists people with the lesson of universal love. This spirit may decide to return to earth for the purpose of serving humanity. Mother Theresa is a likely example of a soul who incarnated for the purpose of humanitarian service, as was the soul who embodied itself as Mohandas Gandhi.

Personal Experiences

The Bible talks about the "quickening of the flesh" which occurs when the Spirit is near. When I was in my twenties I was re-introduced to my Spirit Guides in this physical way. I had previously heard of them as Guardian Angels when I attended Catholic primary school. When I was seven or eight years old, I used to ask my Guardian Angel to wake me up early on Saturday mornings—without an alarm clock—so that I could watch my favorite cartoons on television. It always worked! I would wake up at whatever time I had decided on. I also used to play school often with my spirit friends. As I grew older, however, I relegated Guardian Angels to the compost heap of childish concepts and forgot about the help they had provided me.

Many years later, six months after I'd had a near-death experience, I attended an introductory workshop on ESP and heard about Guardian Angels again. In this metaphysical context they were called Spirit Guides. One feature of the program of study was a private consultation with a counselor to introduce the individual to a working communication with his or her Guides. I decided to take the plunge. A few days later I was in the consulting room, hearing about my Guides and feeling goosebumps all over my body. The counselor told me that I had five Guides. She assigned each one a place on my body to communicate with me physically through vibrations or chills. One Guide was supposed to touch me on my left leg, one on each arm, one on my head and one on my spine.

After the consultation I began to feel goosebumps on these parts of my body quite frequently. The power of suggestion had worked— I had accepted that it was possible to communicate with Spirit by physical means—my body. My Spirit Guides were willing to reach me within that framework. When I had a spontaneous thought or idea, I would often feel a tingling or a shiver in one or more areas of my body. I also received frequent ringing in my ears when I had a significant thought and I began to see little lights in my field of vision. Through these signals I knew that one or more of my Guides was confirming or validating my thoughts and feelings. In this way, and through meditation and "writing by guidance," I gradually got to know my Guides as personalities, each with his or her own area of expertise.

My Guide Betty touches me on my head—she likes to dance over it sometimes, spreading pleasant vibrations like a miniature Tinkerbell. Her area of expertise is individual counseling and work with small groups. She makes people feel welcome and comfortable, giving them a safe space in which to grow at their own pace. My Guide Nathan touches me on my right hand and forearm. Nathan is a healer, not only of the body, but of ideas about reality, both on an individual and a mass level. He and I were Jewish Kabbalists together, long ago.

I remember an incident with my Guides which occurred during a period of great stress in my life. I was coming home one evening after leading a meditation group in Milwaukee, about a hundred miles from my home. As I relaxed into my seat on the Greyhound bus, I wondered if it were worthwhile for me to do "spiritual work" when my personal life was in such chaos. As I relaxed deeper I began to feel the pleasant tingling sensation with which I was so familiar, but more intense than ever before! It was my Guide Betty reassuring me that I was doing good and appropriate work, and that my Guides supported my role as a group facilitator. At that moment I experienced a healing as I sat back and enjoyed the fruits of my labor. I felt intense tingling for an hour and a half—all the way home. What welcome ecstasy!

In the initial consultation where I met my Guides, I learned a technique to use my body to get "yes" and "no" answers from them. Later I revised this system to make use of my right arm (see previous chapter). Clear communicating with this technique requires emotional detachment on the part of the practitioner. Body Signals practitioners may find that they feel blockages in areas of the body which reflect areas in the psyche where they feel pressured. The pressure and one's limiting beliefs about a certain subject may hamper the flow of information that is available from one's Guides on that issue. If one has a block about money, he or she will carry that fear into questions about abundance. The fear will distort the clarity of the information the Guides may wish to share. Either the questioner will not ask questions appropriate to the situation or he or she will be too quick to judge the answers, giving up before exploring deeply enough in the search for truth. When one is in the midst of a block, one may need to simply pose the question to the universe and let it go. The answer may come later at a time when one least expects it, when the body is more relaxed. Perhaps the Guides will slip in a message when one has asked about something completely different.

Body Signals and Spirit Guides

When we pick up non-physical signals around our bodies, it reminds us that we too are Spirit, that most of our so-called human reality is non-physical. The universal law states that like attracts like. Our Guides have chosen to be with us because they resonate to us and our lessons.

A being who is experiencing Oneness, or the Light, will have a much faster vibration than one that experiences separation. When we need encouragement our vibration will probably resonate at a slower pace than when we are in bliss. Then our Guides' energy will probably be felt as a vibration distinct from our own, as a literal "quickening of the flesh." When we are already at peace, our Guides' energy does not seem so distinct from ours. Their energies may enter our energy field, deliver a subtle message and move on freely, leaving no imprint, just a residue of peace and encouragement.

Usually our communication with our Spirit Friends is on a much clearer, yet subtler level than the dramas we play out in our human relationships. In this culture we are taught to think of ourselves as separate beings and that no one can understand our feelings, so we spend a lot of energy explaining and defending ourselves. With our Guides this is unnecessary—they accept us as we are. Finding the divinity within us, they encourage our creativity to flower through a continuous stream of love and feedback from our environment.

To recognize the full purpose of Spirit Guides in our lives, we need to relax into the feeling of fellowship, of comradeship between equals. We must let go of inner guidance as an excuse to feel unequal to and separate from the Source. Our Spirit Guides do not want to be part of such a game—they want to play with us in the Light, as friends.

Testing the Spirits

How can a practitioner of the Body Signals system tell the difference between a Spirit Guide and a confused soul that is trying to intrude? Trust your feelings—Spirit Guides will impart feelings of empowerment, centeredness or serenity. Confused souls will feel like pressure, self-importance or depression. One's Structure Point or Spirit Guide Point on the hand may hurt.

On many occasions my friends and I have worked with souls who have passed on in confusion, to help them find peace. We have seen that not all people on "the other side" know they no longer have physical bodies. Some earthbound souls—that is, people who are stuck in limitation and separation—may try to be helpful to the living, but their effectiveness is limited without the larger perspective of the Light. The Spirit Guide Point at the bottom of the hand in the center, just above the wrist, can be a useful tool to "test the Spirits, whether they are of God." If the Spirit Guide Point gives off a pleasurable sensation, it confirms that you are in communication with guidance. If a constricting pain occurs, cleanse yourself of any outside entities that are lurking in your aura.

Sensing energy at your Spirit Guide Point can be your litmus test to determine whether the guidance is of the Light. Remember that your physical feelings are your ultimate criterion. Once you are satisfied that the Guide is of good intent, then open your aura to the information or healing that this being makes available to you. You may open your body to additional points of contact with your Guides, such as the arms, head or chest, and start feeling tingling sensations there regularly.

It is useful to check in with your inner child before working with transcendent guidance. As a symbol for your memory bank or unconscious mind, your inner child carries memories from many lifetimes. In some of these lives you may have been persecuted, abused or killed in the name of the Higher Power of God or religion. Consequently your inner child may feel mistrustful of anything connected with spiritual authority. In Chapter 4 you learned a technique to get in touch with your inner child by going to a safe place ("sanctuary") in your solar plexus, where no one else can enter without your inner child's permission. This includes your higher self and your Spirit Guides. The purpose of this sanctuary is to provide your inner child with a safe place where a strong sense of self can take root. As you gain a deeper grasp of your personal identity, you will understand that you make the policies and choices that rule your life. You are not a child anymore, being subjected to the choices made for you by the outside world and authority figures.

Because our sense of our true self has been violated so often by the outer circumstances of life, we must take time for self-healing. This way we learn trust in our larger destiny. Our trust in self is the foundation for trust in our Guides and, indeed, for our trust in the vast world outside the personal self. Once a strong trust in self has been established, it will be difficult for us to be led away from our path by con artists and confused souls, whether they be embodied or not.

Life Tasks and Spirit Guides

Some Spirit Guides come into our lives for a limited time, do their work and move on. Some can remain with us for our entire lifetime. Guides who are more task oriented will provide help in a specific area of life we need to learn about. When we have mastered that lesson, or have changed our life plan so that the original lesson is no longer relevant, the Guide for that task will leave our field of energy. Consequently, after we have made major life decisions, we may feel a shift in the spiritual vibrations around our bodies.

My guide Betty has been with me throughout my adult life—the tinglings on my head have remained fairly consistent since my introduction to her twenty years ago. For many years I also had a Guide who touched me on my left leg. For awhile he was the spokesman for my entire team of Guides. He revealed several of his reincarnational aspects to me—Italian priest, Mayan priest-healer, African-American slave and preacher. His function was teaching through preaching and public speaking, and so he helped me a great deal with media appearances and public lecturing. During public speaking engagements I would go into a kind of trance state in which my Guide would lecture or teach through me. Often, after I had completed my presentation, I would have no conscious recall of what I had said—it had all been spoken in trance.

Several years ago while I was meditating, my Guide announced that he was reincarnating on the earth plane to get his own set of vocal chords and speak his own truth. He said that I had mastered what he had come to teach me and that his work with me as my Guide was completed. We would still be friends, of course, communicating through the inner realms of thoughts and feelings.

I was saddened by my Guide's departure for a time, but I understood that I had graduated in some sense—I had completed a part of my life purpose. I stopped feeling the tinglings on my left leg and started feeling them in another part of my body as another Guide came in to take the Preacher's place. Since his departure the most striking difference in my life is that I no longer feel "out of body" while doing public speaking. Instead I work with my Guides consciously as I speak, as part of a team. Since I am more aware of the truth as it is channeled through me, it is easier to integrate it into my own life. In gratitude to my Preacher Guide, I would like to acknowledge that the partnership we experienced together has inspired me with a strong sense of trust in the gifts of the Spirit, as manifested in inspirational speaking.

Everyone makes a life contract with at least one Guide, so that he or she can receive "big picture" support of his or her life purpose. Those whose purpose involves reaching others have more Guides, because we must relate to several points of view in order to communicate with various kinds of people. During a specific period of life we will probably work consciously with only one or two Guides, one Guide acting as "spokespirit" for the team. Guides do not have the ego and personality issues that we do, since they inhabit the so-called "upper astral plane," a relatively unified field of consciousness.

If an entity that calls itself your Guide starts exerting pressure on you to take a particular course of action, it is wise to stop and center yourself, testing the spirit to make sure it is of the Light. If the entity does not inhabit the Light (Christ consciousness, unconditional love), ask your Oversoul and your Spirit Guides for the backing to cast the spirit out of your aura. Coercion is not in the rule book of Spirit Guides.

Exercise: Getting In Touch with Your Guides

It's a good idea to tape record the following technique or have a friend talk you through it.

During this exercise your main focus is to center yourself and enter a deeply relaxed state. To do this it is best to lie down or sit comfortably. I suggest a basic pranayama (yogic) breath: Breathe in for the count of seven, then hold your breath for the same count. Exhale to the count of seven and then hold again for seven. Breathe slowly and deeply, but do not strain. Do this cycle of breathing seven times.

As you inhale, imagine you are pulling in a calming, relaxing light—perhaps violet or light blue. Your cells are filled with this light, and you let go of all tension.

After you have completed seven rounds of conscious breathing, notice the physical sensations that are inside and surrounding your body. Do you feel waves of heat, coolness or tingling? Perhaps you would like to draw these sensations down from the top of your head, using your hands to spread the energy down across your body. Continue to breathe deeply as you move your hands over your body. When you feel tingling sensations on the surface of your skin and in your body, you will know that you are centered in the Light. You are basking in a sea of spiritual love.

When you feel centered, you may choose to ask your Spirit Guides to make themselves known to you. In this exercise our emphasis is to open up to kinesthetic (touch) sensations. You may also receive visual or verbal impressions from your Guides as well.

Now take several deep breaths. Ask your "Main Guide," the spokesperson for the group, to create a tangible presence in your energy field. Your Main Guide may be a spirit with whom you are already familiar, or it may be someone new. Ask this Guide to touch you on the part of your body where he or she wishes to communicate with you. Now breathe into this part of your body and let yourself feel the vibrations. Take your time. Notice: Is this a gentle presence? Is it strong and fearless? Is it a healing energy? Relax and breathe into the presence of your Main Guide.

If you feel it's appropriate, ask your Main Guide to introduce you to another Guide that would like to communicate with you at this time. Breathe slowly and deeply, allowing the feeling of your Guides' presence to expand to another part of your body. You may feel a shift in the vibration of the energy which is washing over your body. Breathe into it and invite your second Guide to manifest for you. You will get a sense of this Guide's area of expertise, as it affects your life. When you are comfortable with your second Guide, ask how he or she and your Main Guide work together.

Then ask each of your Guides, "Have I known you in another lifetime? What was our relationship?" Breathe deeply and allow yourself to relax into the pictures, words and feelings that come, just accepting them and breathing into them.

When you feel ready, ask your Main Guide if there is someone else waiting to be introduced to you, or whether you have made enough contacts for now. If another Guide is available to you, allow that presence to touch you in a specific part of your body. Breathe deeply and allow a special message to come through. When you have received it, integrate your third Guide with your other Guides, and find out how they work together as a team. Trust your intuitive knowing.

You may meet as many Guides as are available to relate to you at this time. Let your feelings tell you when you have done enough for the present moment. At your point of completion, you will relax and feel the presence of your whole team of Guides around you. You will never feel alone again!

To come out of this meditative state, breathe once again according to the "7–7–7–7" pattern: Inhale for the count of seven, hold for seven, exhale for seven, hold again for seven. Do seven rounds of this breathing. As you breathe, allow your Guides to suggest a color you can inhale, that is both relaxing and stimulating. Fill up your cells and tissues with this color. After you have completed the breathing cycle, shake out your hands and feet, get up slowly and stretch. At this point you may want to take some time to make notes of your experiences and to set up another "appointment" to contact your Guides.

Message from My Guides

We speak here as a collective energy. It is time for all of you to receive help in your lives. As a culture you have been too skeptical of where the help is coming from. This suspicion keeps you locked into your existing roles with each other. When someone gives love, it is trans-formative both for the giver and for the recipient(s). When there is acceptance, then it is hard to pigeonhole the giver as a criminal, addict, member of another race or lifestyle. The giver gives, you receive. It is as simple as that, so that love can be expressed easily from one to another.

> *Our role is to be a moving force in your lives at this time, to help you break out of old ruts and phobias. We provide input which can have a quickening effect on your lives. It is not that we have THE TRUTH, but rather that we are open to sharing what we know with others, without holding anything back. When you share in this way you are blessed in a way that transcends material goods.*

> *Do not feel sorry for those in pain, starvation, disease. Rather, help them to fulfill their true desires by connecting them with the Light within. Realignment is spontaneous when a person is connected with the Light. This is true on both an individual and*

a social level. This means that political turbulence will shift if nourishment of the spirit is provided for. Many may choose to go on out of body, but the main thing is that they will be on their path to wholeness. Your journey does not stop with what you call death. We do not place the same finality on death that you do. Nevertheless, we support your attempts to build a happier life for all on earth—this is a true soul desire on your part. Inevitably deep soul desires must be satisfied. Your task is to find out what motivates you the most deeply, and to follow that dream.

The earth is a living body. We cannot stress this enough. As you treat the earth as a living consciousness like yourself, you will lose your sense of alienation and the fear that you do not belong on this planet. Peace to you all!

Do Angels Have Gender?
Do They Really Dance on the Head of a Pin?

Because they are not in physical bodies, our Guides, strictly speaking, do not have gender, which is a function only of the physical plane. However, Guides will usually relate to us through the filter of one or more of their lives on earth as human beings. Most Guides have experienced many earth lives, developing preferences for certain occupations, lifestyles and gender identification. However, I learned from my Preacher Guide that it was easy for him to change his image at will—all he needed to do was to change his thoughts: This changed the reality that he projected to my mind.

During one meditation we may see a beautiful woman in white, flowing robes while we feel a tingling on our right shoulder. The next day during meditation we may feel the same warm tingling on our shoulder, but instead of the beautiful woman we see an inner picture of a burly male truck driver! "What gives?" we may ask. Our Spirit Friend may reply that he/she is trying to wean us away from personal stereotyping in our relationship to inner guidance.

I remember one incisive example of my Guides breaking up my angelic stereotypes. I was meditating to contact my Guides as a group. My Preacher Guide had come to fetch me—we floated up, up, up to the Source, our rendezvous point with the whole cadre. Much to my surprise, I arrived to find a bunch of tough-looking characters playing cards, drinking whiskey and smoking cigars. "These can't be my Guides!?" I exclaimed. One fellow put his cards face down, turned around from his place at the table and said, "Don't bother me; this is a good hand!" I got the message from this experience that my Guides would not allow me to keep them on a pedestal any longer. They let me know that they were just characters who liked a good time, like me!

Message from Nathan

Nathan is my Healing Guide.

Make your Guides into a game! Pretend that wherever you go, we accompany you. You can talk to us, tell us your problems and viewpoints. When you have shared all you want with us, you may be open to listen to what we have to say to you. Remember, this is not a one-way communication, from us to you. We are interested in your experiences also—we grow through communication with you.

When you are used to having us around, you will notice that you see things differently, from a new perspective. It is as though you have the perspective of several beings inside of you. Each one complements the others—there is no need to fear competition among your Guides. We are friendly, but not usually intrusive, unless you really need it: Then consider it a friendly tap on the shoulder.

Most of all, do not hide your talents. The world has much need of them right now, and you have spent lifetimes perfecting them. As you let them out more, you attract your Good to you more forcefully. We let you make your own mistakes, but we do not want you to grope around in darkness unnecessarily. Let the Light in, and be happy.

—◄o►—

We are never alone. Communicating with guidance has provided practitioners of Body Signals with abundant assurance of this fact. The inner certainty of our connectedness has grown as we have opened ourselves to the stream of messages that comes to us everyday. The concept of spiritual guidance is not just for Sunday mornings, but is meant to be integrated into every activity. Paying attention to the body signals sent by our Guides can save us a lot of unnecessary worry, while illustrating the truth that we live in a vast sea of thoughts and feelings, all interconnected in a master grid.

CHAPTER SEVEN

Body Signals and the Tree of Life

Often known as the yoga of the West, the Jewish spiritual tradition of the Kabbalah is a tool for knowledge of the divine nature of the self. My students and I have found it beneficial to integrate a template of body signals with the Kabbalistic mandala (symbol) called the Tree of Life. We feel signals in our bodies in a Tree of Life pattern. This tool has assisted us in our quest for greater psychic sensitivity in a context of self-awareness. This chapter will outline the basic framework of the Tree of Life and will show how we can use the Body Signals concept in still another way to get in touch with our intuitive self.

The Tree of Life in the Body

The Kabbalistic mandala of the Tree of Life contains ten centers of consciousness, called *sephiroth* in Hebrew ("Lights"), connected by twenty-two pathways of energy. The accompanying illustrations show how the Tree of Life can be studied within the human body, so that the ten sephiroth and the twenty-two pathways vibrate within the physical body itself.

At this point, as we begin ascribing centers to the right and left sides of the body, remember that the physical placement of the centers can vary, depending on the neurological makeup of the person using the system. A practitioner might be left-handed, or what the Native American Lakota people call *heyoka*—contrary, having energy that flows opposite the usual. The right side and left side pillars of the Tree of Life would then be reversed for that person. Also, one's experience with the centers in the body can shift, depending on one's frame of mind or emotional state in that moment. One might find that the right side of the body has temporarily become the creative side, while the left has adopted more rational associations. By tuning into our body consciousness during meditation, we can discern the psychic functioning of each part of our physical mechanism. Our experience of right/left polarities can change, depending on the influences we receive into our consciousness.

Three Centers of Divinity

Looking at the diagrams, we see that the sephira (center) called *Kether* in Hebrew (I will call it *Unity*) is located at the top of the head. Its traditional English name is *Crown*. The sephira *Chokhmah, the Impulse to Create*, is located at the right side of the head. Its traditional English name is *Wisdom. Binah, the Void or the Great Mother Womb*, is found at the left side of the head. Its traditional English name is *Understanding*.

These top three sephiroth (centers), Kether, Chokhmah and Binah, are sometimes called the Supernal triangle, because they represent three aspects of divinity: Unity (Kether), male (Chokhmah) and

The Tree of Life: The Sephiroth

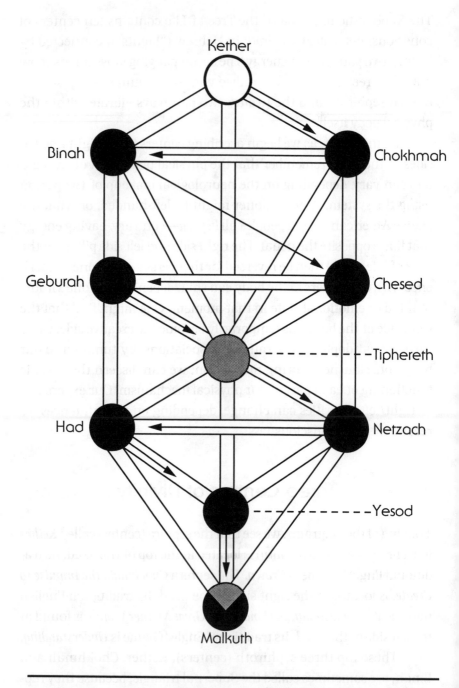

Kether

Binah

Chokhmah

Geburah

Chesed

Tiphereth

Had

Netzach

Yesod

Malkuth

———▶ = *The Lightning Flash of Creation*

female (Binah). Kether is traditionally associated with the color white; Chokhmah, with gray and Binah, with black. The planet traditionally associated with the Binah center is Saturn. Chokhmah is associated with the entire Zodiac, while Kether transcends the physical universe as we know it.

Unity

My own experience with Kether, the center of Unity consciousness, is connected to the opening of my own consciousness to the love and caring of Spirit. I often feel my crown chakra buzzing with pleasant tinglings from my Guide Betty, who loves to dance at the top of my head. She reminds me of my unity with "the big picture," especially when I am involved with group or counseling activities, which are her areas of focus.

In the lives of Body Signals practitioners Kether acts as a gateway center to non-physical portions of reality. In meditation, practitioners often feel strong tingling sensations at the top of the head when they merge with their Oversoul, the composite self, including all physical lifetimes.

The Kether sephira became activated for me in a new way in 1979 when I allowed my higher self to open a conduit of energy to my conscious personality. This happened during a conference where my spiritual teacher was present. I had been feeling a pressure at the top of my head gradually building over a period of months. I felt the presence of a new type of consciousness, but I was afraid to let it in because of the extensive work I was doing on healing souls in confusion—I was afraid that the energy was malignant and wanted to "possess" me. In the presence of my teacher I decided it was safe to let the energy come into my body, thinking that he could cast it out if it was not of the Light. I took a deep breath and let the energy rush in through the top of my head. Much to my surprise I felt a surge of ecstasy filling my entire body! I understood that this pressure was my higher self's desire to merge with my physical body—I felt a new level of wholeness. My teacher noticed the brightness of my aura, and this reassured me about

The Tree of Life in the Body

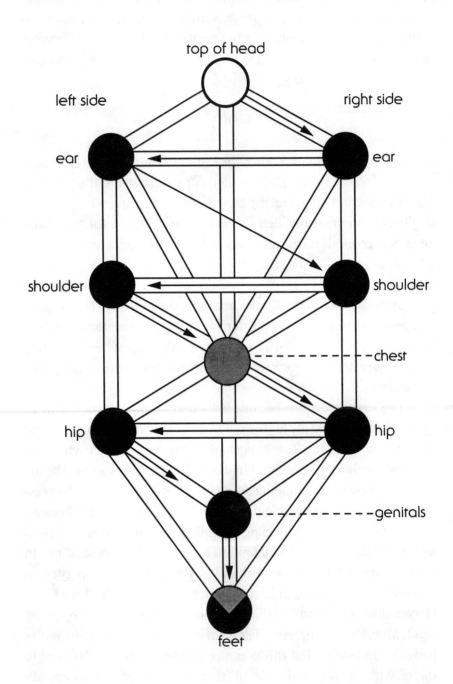

the validity of my experience. My integration signaled the completion of my student/teacher agreement with him—he had led me to experience my own Unity.

Since this experience I have undertaken the quest to be my own teacher. I find the more I teach others, the more effective is my inner leadership of myself. I acknowledge the Universe and all sentient beings within as my teachers of the moment. I am also conscious of the fact that I must not give my power away to any authority figure outside myself. It is good to remember that all sentient beings have a Kether center, an access point to unity with their own personal truth.

The Impulse to Create

Chokhmah, or the Impulse to Create, is the center of consciousness of the limitless outpouring of ideas from Source. When the right ear or right side of the head is buzzing and tingling, it means that the higher self wants our attention to give us ideas about new projects, plans and potentialities. These will be entertained for awhile and then sorted out in the next center of divinity, Binah. This is analogous to the male and female roles in the act of procreation—the father sends out millions of sperm (ideas from Source) to fertilize a single one of the mother's eggs (physical structure).

Pain on the right side of the head may be a signal from our male divinity center warning us to not let the creative flow of ideas pass us by. Learn to dream! Let go into the creative flow without the nagging voice saying, "Is it practical?"

The Great Mother

The Binah center, or Great Mother, is often activated for Body Signals practitioners by a pronounced ringing in the left ear. This signal creates the mental space (womb) for the practitioner to receive information from Source in a safe way where ideas can gestate and grow. This illustrates Binah's function as feminine (receptive) divinity.

The left side of the head may tingle and vibrate as a signal for us to surrender to the Void within ourselves, the black hole of consciousness where we have no preconceptions about our truth. The Divine Mother asks us to cast our fears into the Void so that we can accept the support of the Universe in this moment. Surrendering to the Void may feel like a death experience, but it is essential in the cycle of life so that new forms may develop.

The Ethical Triangle

Practitioners of Body Signals Kabbalah find that all the centers of consciousness on the Tree of Life become activated as they open to the inner promptings of their Soul. Moving downward on the Tree, we encounter the next three centers, called the Ethical Triangle because they address our relationship to interpersonal situations. In descending order, their names are *Chesed* (*Mercy*), *Geburah* (*Judgment*) and *Tiphereth* (*Essence*; traditionally called *Beauty*). In the Body Signals system Chesed is located in the right shoulder, Geburah in the left shoulder and Tiphereth in the esoteric heart center in the middle of the chest. In Kabbalistic tradition Chesed is associated with the planet Jupiter—its color is blue. Geburah is associated with Mars—its color is red. Tiphereth is associated with the sun—its color is gold. We can think of each one of these centers as an attribute of God, or Source, as it manifests in our human relationships with the world. In the case of Geburah (Judgment), Judaeo-Christian tradition states that no one but God is permitted to judge. How then can we as humans apply judgment correctly? When we make choices that affect others we must rise above our personal likes and dislikes, applying the positive qualities of discrimination and fairness. They act as a kind of weeding out process to find our true motives. When we act from our core truth we can be confident that our decisions are for the highest good of others as well as ourselves.

Similarly, as spiritual seekers we do not base our application of mercy on personal whim, but rather because we realize we have an opportunity to let more love and light into the situation. Mercy could take the form of opening our heart to make a new friend, to replace an old but well-beloved car, to search for a new house or to consider new career options. We also apply the Mercy center when we expand our consciousness to include new ways of looking at life philosophically, letting go of old prejudices.

Personal Story: Mercy in Action

For a period of several weeks I had an inflammation in my right shoulder area, extending down from my neck to my right shoulderblade. This inflammation became so painful that I had trouble sleeping, so I went to a chiropractor who also was trained in acupuncture. His treatments helped enormously—after the third one I walked out of his office pain free! But at the moment I realized that the pain was gone, a wave of resentment washed over me. I heard the thought, "How dare he remove my pain!" and in that moment the pain returned full force.

Clearly, I thought, I hadn't dealt with the underlying cause of the inflammation. I decided to breathe into the pain and ask it what it was trying to tell me. With deep clarity I heard the words, "father issues." Later in meditation I searched deeper for additional insight and received the following impression: I was signing my name to an agreement to buy a new car, and the pain was gone!

Intuitively I knew that this was a true impression, although my rational mind had trouble accepting its direct simplicity. As an urban person I had been without a car for several years. Lately I'd thought I needed a car to increase my mobility, so that I could teach workshops and classes in other states more easily. Buying a new car was not a financial burden. My main block was the trauma I still carried about my father's terrible history with cars, including several brushes with death. I had carried this pattern into my adult life with the two previous cars I had owned, taking unnecessary risks and driving them when they were mechanically unsafe. Now that I had an opportunity to own a brand new vehicle I was ready to release my father's "carma" and expand my own horizons. This was a form of mercy shown to self, thus the right shoulder issue.

I realized that out of a fear of repeating my father's patterns, I had been blocking the abundance (mercy) of the Universe in its attempt to meet my needs. My emotional fear was the cause of the right shoulder inflammation. Having grasped this I moved quickly to purchase a new car (and get rid of the pain!). Just as predicted, as I put my name on the owner's agreement the pain completely vanished and the inflammation did not return.

This experience taught me that I must expand my framework of awareness in order for the Universe to support me abundantly. The process of expanding into my good is the Mercy center at work.

Judgment

I have been shown many times that the proper use of the center Geburah (Judgment) does not involve being judgmental. I remember sitting in the front row during a church service, listening as the priest gave a sermon. Suddenly a brilliant golden light appeared around his head—it remained for several minutes. Then the priest began to berate the congregation for their closed attitude toward newcomers. As he projected his anger out onto the congregation, I saw his aura change from gold to black. A black energy field remained around him until he changed his tone at the end of the sermon. As he closed with words of love, the priest's aura was restored to its golden hue, as bright as before.

I did not usually see colors in the aura so brightly, so I asked my Guides why this vision had been shown to me. They replied, "*So that you can see what happens to your aura when **you** become judgmental.*" I understood from this experience that the priest communicated his message of friendliness and inclusiveness more effectively when his aura was golden than when it was black; that is, when he was coming from centered essence rather than a judgmental attitude.

With the proper use of Judgment, we will not use threats on ourselves or others to get what we want. The use of threats or pressure is like leaning over our plants, breathing heavily and yelling **"grow!"** It has a reverse effect. What Judgment really involves is setting priorities—taking the time and energy to discern what we want and what we don't want in our lives, based on our experience of our inner womb (Binah).

Essence

In Christian, Jewish and Muslim mysticism, the heart center is a symbol of our unique consciousness as human beings. In the Kabbalistic system of self-knowledge the heart center usually matches with Tiphereth (Beauty), which I call the Essence center. Tiphereth is not located at the organ of the heart, but rather in the center of the chest. When this center is open and resonating, we are living lives as full human beings expressing our potential.

Tiphereth symbolizes the expression of our true nature as souls in flesh. Sometimes it is called the Christ or Messiah center because it acts as a bridge between the five aspects of divinity above it and the four earthly aspects below it on the Tree of Life. As you activate your essence expression in new ways, you may feel an expanding pain in your sternum, as if your breastbone were growing larger. I do not advocate ignoring pain as a warning signal. Nevertheless, I feel that this type of expanding pain is a symptom of **personal growth**, not illness.

If you are used to interpreting pain as a warning signal from the body, you may have an immediate reaction of worry or fear. When you feel pain, I suggest you breathe into that part of your body and ask the pain for a message about its purpose in your life at this time. Make an effort to avoid being judgmental (closed) about your body signals, labeling them as "good" or "bad."

Like most people, I used to automatically interpret pain signals in a psychologically negative way. More than once I felt a sharp pain in my chest as I became involved in a new relationship. After I began to consciously work with the Body Signals system, I realized that pain was a symbol of the opening of my heart center to give and receive love.

The Ethical Triangle Meditation

This is a meditation to connect the three ethical triangle centers: Chesed (Mercy), Geburah (Judgment) and Tiphereth (Essence). In the human body this means creating pathways of energy between the right and left shoulders, and between each shoulder and the middle of the chest. We will use the traditional colors associated with the centers—gold for Tiphereth, blue for Chesed and red for Geburah.

I recommend that you record this meditation first and play it back for yourself, or get a friend to read it from this book and talk you through it.

Let's begin the meditation by lying down comfortably and breathing deeply. Pause. Now take several minutes to do seven rounds of breathing in the pattern of seven. Inhale to the count of seven; hold the breath for the count of seven; exhale to the count of seven and hold the breath for seven counts. This is one round. Do seven rounds of this breathing. (Pause.) Notice the differences in your body sensations as you inhale, exhale and hold your breath.

When you have completed seven rounds of this breath, focus your attention on the middle of your chest. As you continue to breathe deeply, you will begin to see or feel a golden light there. This light slowly grows into a golden ball, filling your chest cavity. (Pause.)

Continue to breathe deeply. Soon you will feel a ray of energy traveling from your chest to your right shoulder. (Pause.) Breathe into it, feeling the energy moving back and forth between these two areas, the chest and the right shoulder. (Pause.)

When you feel ready, focus your attention on a soft blue light in your right shoulder. Let this light grow in radiance and intensity. Intensify the light by repeating the word

MERCY to yourself slowly, several times. (Pause.) Feelings of expansion wash over your being, along with a light blue light. (Pause.) Notice how your body is feeling—you may feel warmth, coolness, tingling or goosebumps, or other sensations. (Pause.) Which body signals are you experiencing right now?

Now take your awareness back to the golden light in the center of your chest. You can **feel** the presence of the golden light. Repeat this word intently to yourself: *ESSENCE, ESSENCE, ESSENCE,* letting it resound within your chest cavity. (Pause.) Feel the golden rays of light expanding out from your heart center. (Pause.)

When you feel ready, shift your focus to your left shoulder, the red center of Judgment. You will now begin to feel a pathway of energy connecting your left shoulder with the middle of your chest. (Pause.) Directing your attention back to your left shoulder, breathe a red light into it, and repeat the word *JUDGMENT* several times. Notice the effect this affirmation has on you. (Pause.) Now you will begin to feel a contraction of energy in your left shoulder—not an unpleasant constriction, but a feeling of definite structure and boundaries. (Pause.)

At your own pace, shift your focus of attention from one center to another: From the heart center, to the right shoulder, to the left shoulder and back again to the heart. (Pause.)

Notice the change in your body sensations as you move from center to center. Remember to breathe deeply. (Pause.) Try not to have a prejudice for or against any particular center, but move equally among them.

Now allow each center to give you a message that relates to your life at this time. (Pause.)

When each center has delivered its message for today, start drawing your meditation to a close. Breathe deeply, spreading golden light throughout your body, focusing your attention on your Essence center in the chest. (Pause.) If you like, chant several deep *OHM's* to bring the exercise to completion. (Pause.) When you are ready, sit up and stretch.

The Personality Triangle

The lowest four centers on the Tree of Life describe aspects of our life in the world of individual reality.

Appreciation

I call the center in the lower right pillar the *Appreciation* center; its Hebrew name is *Netzach*; its traditional occult name is *Victory*. In the Body Signals system this center is located in the right hip area of the body. (See diagram.) The Appreciation center quickens our aesthetic sense through acknowledgment of beauty and art. It also marks cycles and transitions with ritual—birth, death, marriage, change of location, harvest and so forth. In Kabbalistic lore the planet Venus, associated with the goddess of love, beauty and sensuality, rules this center. Its color is green.

In working with the Appreciation center our inner child connects to higher self with a sense of awe and gratitude, a feeling of being part of something larger than itself. In this spirit we create rituals of wholeness that strengthen our sense of life's continuity over time. We co-create a safe space for our values, our hopes, our creative expression and our loved ones. We allow ourselves to spend time and energy creating an environment that is both beautiful and nurturing. We value what is psychically durable, that is, based on deep-seated values, whether personal or learned.

The Appreciation center connects us with the social collective, with its rules and traditions. When working with this center of consciousness, the individual will accept the social context and work with it creatively, building on what already exists.

Craft

In the left hip area we find the *Craft* center, which rules all conscious thought processes; its Hebrew name is *Hod*, its traditional English name *Splendor*. It is ruled by the planet Mercury, which is associated with communication; its color is orange.

Our conscious mind provides structure for our worldview and an incentive to find personal applications for theoretical concepts. It is in charge of the safety of the inner child on an everyday basis, reconfiguring perceptions continuously so that what happens makes sense to the personality.

The Craft center is found on the feminine side (left side) of the Tree of Life, while the Appreciation center lies on the masculine side (right side). This placement corresponds with many earth traditions, such as the Hawaiian, which ascribe the role of nurturing mother to the conscious mind. The Craft center helps us to focus on what needs to be done in the moment so that our instincts can flow freely and without impediments. Daily routines for health (exercise, yoga, etc.) and well-being (journaling, meditation) come within the bailiwick of the Craft center, as we regularly clear our mind and our aura of energy that is no longer needed for clear functioning.

Imagination

The center Yesod, or *Imagination*, is located in the lower abdomen of the body, just above the scrotum in a man, and in a woman's vaginal area. It is the astral creative center, in which the personality lives in an inner world of its own making before those thoughts and feelings become outer circumstances in physical reality. Its traditional English name is *Foundation*; it is ruled by the moon, changeable and emotional. Yesod's color is violet.

This center brings forth our inner reality as a kind of psychic climate or personal envelope which contains our hopes and fears, dreams and aspirations. Often these are unconscious, and consequently our emotional state takes us by surprise; or we may find that our lives are richer in the dream state than in the waking state. Our task is to integrate our unconscious drives and desires as much as possible with our conscious direction in life.

Manifestation

The center that represents the outside physical world is called in Hebrew *Malkuth*. Its traditional name in English is *Kingdom*—I call it *Manifestation*. In the Body Signals system the Manifestation center is located in the feet, which provide the underpinnings to our physical reality. Foot reflexology tells us that the feet contain pressure points connected to each organ of the body. In the same way, the Manifestation center provides a synthesis for all the centers on the Tree of Life: The aspects of Force (right side), Form (left side) and direct experience (Middle Pillar) as the life force travels from the ultimate Unity in Kether, to the ultimate diversity of the physical plane in Malkuth. Four traditional earth tones are associated with this center—russet red, citrine yellow, olive green and black.

We may program ourselves to activate body signals in any of the areas of the body which are associated with the Tree of Life. For the ten sephiroth, or states of being, this would include the top of the head, the right and left sides of the head and the ears, the right and left shoulders and hips, the chest, the genitals and the feet. Now let us consider the dynamic creative processes as they connect the body with the Tree of Life.

The Twenty-Two Pathways

Traditionally there are twenty-two pathways that connect the ten centers of being (sephiroth) on the Tree of Life. The tradition of Tarot card divination is based on these pathways. (See diagram.) Each path on the Tree of Life corresponds to one face (Major Arcana) card. The symbolism of Tarot can be a valuable perspective to enhance our

The 22 Pathways of the Tree of Life and the Major Arcana of the Tarot

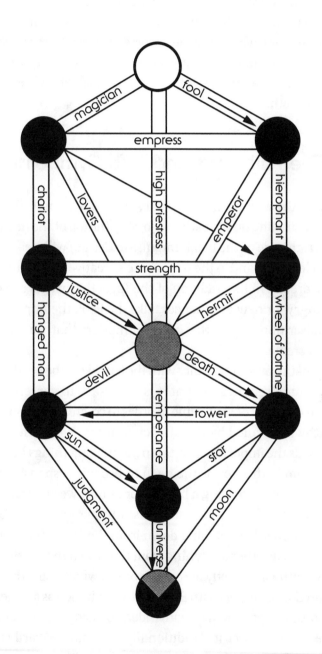

understanding of Kabbalah, helping us to use it as a practical self-awareness tool.

We can train each of the twenty-two pathways to send us body signals when we are engaged in activities that relate to that particular path. We will find that the pathways relate more to specific actions and dynamic changes, while the centers correlate with states of consciousness such as imagination, expansion and focus. Kabbalistic pathways act as a bridge between the states of being which are woven together as the sephiroth.

The Pathways and Tarot Symbolism

The first pathway joins Kether (Unity) with Chokhmah (Impulse to Create). Meditating on the pathway joining the top of the head (Unity) with the right side of the head (Impulse to Create) will clear the mental obstacles that stand in the way of one's creative imagination, one's ability to dream. In the tradition of the Tarot this path is ruled by the Fool, hungry for new experiences. Like the Fool, the Impulse to Create is indiscriminate—in this center it matters that you create, not **what** you create.

The pathway joining Unity with the left side of the head, the black Void of Binah, reminds us that it is necessary to surrender to the unknown quantity of **God's time** in order to co-create our own reality. This pathway is ruled by the Magician in the Tarot; the Magician understands the importance of timing in making things happen. We can program both sides of the head to become responsive to these psychic energies, providing a barometer of how we are accepting the various aspects of Unity into our conscious life. We might feel a tingling line of energy stretching down from the top of the head to the right ear, and another stretching from the crown to the left ear.

The pathway directly across the brain, which joins the Impulse to Create (God as Father) with Binah the Womb (God as Mother), helps us to choose one particular creative idea, focusing on it sufficiently to nurture and empower it. Traditionally the Empress card rules this pathway—she symbolizes fecundity and fertility, as we allow our unconscious to be fertilized by the creative inflow of ideas, while focusing the limitless outpouring of our imagination so that specific forms can develop. In the Womb center we allow the idea (zygote) to gestate until the time is right for it to emerge into the mental planning stage. This dynamic pathway represents the actions that need to be taken so that the chosen idea can get the nurturing it needs to develop properly. The Empress will water her garden and protect it from harm. The pathway joining the masculine and feminine sides of divinity illustrates the process of moving from an indiscriminate outpouring of many ideas, to a selective focus on one.

Discussing the pathways in descending order down the Tree, we see from the diagram that the Emperor connects the Impulse to Create with the heart center of Tiphereth, Essence. The Emperor gives us the courage, the inner authority to embody and live out our dreams. In the physical body, this pathway would connect the right side of the head with the chest. The corresponding pathway on the left side of the body is ruled by the Lovers, who symbolize conscious partnership as we make agreements based on both spiritual understanding (Binah) and personal truth (Essence). We can use this pathway to release our heart's desire back to the Source (Womb), to gestate there and be born again at the appropriate time.

The High Priestess officiates in bringing down the universal truth of Kether (Unity) to the personal realm of Essence, from the top of the head down to the chest. The Hierophant (High Priest) brings down God's mercy from the Impulse to Create, to the Mercy center where we apply it ethically to our relationships in society. The Chariot, connecting the Void with Judgment, symbolizes the force with which we emerge from the womb as from a birth canal, focusing our attention on Divine Will as it chooses to manifest in our lives.

The Strength card, ruling the path that connects Mercy and Judgment, reminds us that the challenge is not to get stuck in either polarity. This pathway runs across the so-called upper heart chakra of unconditional love. The Hermit pathway shows how we as humans can stay connected to essence through divine compassion (Mercy), lighting the way for the evolution of the species. Justice is Judgment applied ethically by Essence. In the body, this pathway flows from left shoulder to heart and back again. All these pathways allow energy to flow in both directions, down toward manifestation and up toward Source.

On the right side of the Tree of Life, the Pillar of Mercy, the Wheel of Fortune card connects Mercy and Appreciation. This card symbolizes our personal relationship to our good as we perceive it through cultural and environmental influences. Our culture empowers certain creative channels, considering them important to society, while disempowering others. An example might be the skill of the surgeon versus the skill of the shaman in the arena of healing. The Wheel of Fortune influences the choices we make to create happiness, and what kind of rituals we develop to honor the passages of life (birth, death, beginnings and endings, marriages and dissolutions).

On the left side of the Tree, the Pillar of Severity, the Hanged Man reminds us to take the time for stillness and silence—this empowers us to use good Judgment as we create routines and structures to empower ourselves in daily life (Craft). The Devil symbol warns us of the abuse of power and reminds us to come from the heart while creating forms to support our goals. On this pathway we see the dynamic sorting process of essence seeking to empower its human personality. In my opinion, the Devil card has been associated with this pathway because self-interest has had a bad name in our Western spiritual tradition. The corresponding path on the Mercy (right) side of the Tree is ruled by the Death card, bringing up another prominent fear in our society. The card reminds us of the ultimate passage, death. It also implies that we must let go of control in order for our essence to freely manifest as art and beauty. Our essence creates rituals as there is a need for them, often because of loss or suffering. A funeral, for example, is meant to ennoble a person's life and connect it to essence. Appreciation emerges from the letting go process as we understand that there is no death, only transformation and evolution.

Perhaps the three most feared cards in the tarot deck, The Devil, Death and the Tower, are ascribed to the Personality Triangle on the Tree of Life (Appreciation, Craft, Imagination) to remind us of the ephemeral nature of our creation on the physical plane. The Tower connects Craft and Appreciation. In Body Signals terms, this pathway runs across the lower abdomen, connecting the two hips, joining the rational mind (Craft) with the emotional mind (Appreciation). The Tower card reminds us to look for our strength within, regardless of outside circumstances, by trusting our gut feelings. We must let go of traditions for inventive breakthroughs to occur, discarding outmoded structures as we get the feeling impulses to do so.

Returning to the Middle Pillar, the Temperance card connects Tiphereth with Yesod, Essence with Imagination, the heart with the genitals. This reminds us that our soul desires to "remember itself" as we manifest our desires through Imagination. Given our own particular value system, we will live in balance as we let our soul work through us. The heart center, Tiphereth, is our direct connection to Soul.

The Star connects the genitals with the right hip (Imagination with Appreciation). We use our imagination to remember our universal origins, creating rituals and art to commemorate them. We would activate this pathway while contemplating the beauty of a work of art, or by visualizing it in our mind. Imagining the technical steps needed to create the piece would activate the corresponding pathway on the left side of the body, ruled by the Sun, shedding the light of our conscious mind on our creative imagination.

The Tarot card Judgment rules the lowermost pathway on the left side of the Tree of Life, the Pillar of Severity. This path connects Craft with Manifestation, the left hip down through the left leg to the feet. With Judgment, we decide what will be manifested and what will be transmuted or discarded. The systems of behavior that we create in the Craft center are what produce our external reality.

On the other side of the Tree, the pathway down the right leg connects Appreciation with Manifestation; it is ruled by the Moon. This gives us respect for the cyclical nature of reality, an awareness that Divine Mercy comes in waves—it is not constant, though ever-present.

Finally, the path connecting the genitals with the feet, Imagination with Manifestation, is ruled by the Universe card. In this context I would take this card to mean the physical universe which we create as human beings. This card reminds us that all things are possible, based on the inner work we have done further up the Tree. The Tarot symbols remind us that we learn through both change and stability;

through conscious desire and letting go. The Tarot symbols on each of the three pillars represent pathways to actualize our knowledge of the God within us and to bring this power forth in our daily lives. The High Priestess, Temperance and the Universe are symbols of our direct experience of God. The Chariot, the Hanged Man, Judgment—knowledge of God through form, learning when to plunge ahead and when to let go. The Hierophant, the Wheel of Fortune, the Moon—seeing divine mercy in all circumstances, in new moon beginnings and in full moon manifestations.

Practical Use of the Pathways

We can program our bodies to use this system of Kabbalistic and Tarot symbolism for self-awareness. According to this paradigm the left leg is connected to the Tarot card Judgment, the right leg to the Moon. As we study Tarot symbolism, we may find that our body gives us messages which relate to these symbols.

To illustrate, let's link two paradigms together, the inner child and Kabbalah. We find that the Inner Child Point in the body, the left side of the stomach, is related to the Devil path on the Tree of Life, joining heart to left hip. This points to the fear of instincts which is deeply ingrained in our culture, but also reminds us that one of the lessons of the inner child is to learn to use power wisely. In our culture the Devil symbolizes the abuse of power, which is a danger each of us faces as we progress in understanding. Rather than a symbol of absolute evil, the Devil is more properly a warning that fertile circumstances for the abuse of power are present. When our Inner Child Point is hurting, either on the hand or in the stomach, it may be a warning that we perceive our survival to be threatened on a deep level. "Love casts out fear," so our first priority must be to love our inner child, fears and all. Then we can trust that our power drives come from our core essence (heart).

◄o►

I had surgery for an inguinal hernia on the right side of my abdomen. The suture was made at the site of scar tissue which had never healed properly and, once again, the tissue did not heal properly after the surgery. I realized I needed to take a look at some deeper issues so that an effective healing could take place as new tissue formed.

As soon as I made a commitment to look into this life pathway (Appreciation to Imagination), my relationships started to shift. People who wanted me to rescue them dropped out of my life. Consequently I had more time and energy to spend expressing my creative imagination artistically. In doing my inner work I created the emotional ambiance necessary to bring creative projects to fruition. I remembered that a previous surgery had opened up the creative channel on my left side, connecting Craft and Imagination, necessary to clear the negative patterns getting in the way of writing this book. In order to sustain enthusiasm, I also had to clear the right side path between Imagination and Appreciation. Now when I have pain in this area (right lower abdomen) I take it as a warning signal that I am being co-dependent, doing for others what they are capable of doing for themselves.

Empaths, people who have highly developed intuition and feeling, often pick up on the physical symptoms of friends, clients, even complete strangers! This is a mirroring mechanism which reminds us that we are all One. By breathing into the symptoms or the pain that we are channeling, we will get clarity on the aspect of our own consciousness that needs healing.

This was underscored on a visit to friends in my beloved New Mexico a few years ago. As the evening wore on, I became increasingly distressed by a pain in the left part of my groin. Since the surgery there I'd been pain-free in that area, so I wondered what was going on. Was I channeling the issues of my friends? They began to share their concerns about finding a niche in their new community. They did not see how their talents and skills could provide them with a good living there. During a deep group channeling it became apparent that, indeed, the pain was not my own—when I came out of trance it was gone! I realized that my body had been somatizing the Tree of Life, by sensing my friends' blockage on the pathway joining Imagination (groin) and Craft (left hip), ruled by the Sun, self-expression. The issue was: How can I effectively express my creativity in the world, make a living and be respected? The conscious minds of my friends needed input from Spirit so that they could feel secure with the path they had chosen.

Each of us can practice noticing what's going on in our bodies along the pathways joining the Tree of Life centers (sephiroth). The above meditation on the Ethical Triangle (heart center, right and left shoulders) may provide a springboard for new pathway awareness. Remember that the pathways reflect a dynamic flow in consciousness, while the centers reflect a gestalt or energy structure. The next time you feel an energy flow traveling from your chest to your right shoulder, realize that you are connecting a state of expansion (Mercy) with your essence. You might be in the process of setting up a new business venture, or forgiving old debts so that you can move on. The sensation may feel like a cool breeze or a release of pressure. There are many ways that Mercy and Essence can interact—the context of your activities will provide clues for the proper interpretation of your body signals.

The Three Pillars of the Tree of Life

As mentioned above, we can see in the diagrams that there are three distinct "pillars" of Kabbalistic centers. The left-side pillar is known as the Pillar of Severity or the Path of Form. The right side is called the Pillar of Mercy or the Path of Force. The middle column is called the Middle Pillar or the Path of Balance. Each pillar is associated with a distinct approach to self-knowledge. The Pillar of Severity, sometimes called the "lefthand path," is the path of the magician, a person who uses universal laws consciously to create results. The magician says, "I AM GOD: I create _____ as my own reality." In order to be effective, the magician must have knowledge of the proper tools (Craft), impartial Judgment and space in consciousness for new ideas to develop and take form (Womb).

We generally find that the Pillar of Severity affects the left side of the body, usually considered the feminine side. In this context feminine means a kind of responsiveness, using the conscious mind to decide which elements and influences will remain in the aura and which will be discarded. The Pillar of Severity receives input from the other two pillars and selects the forms that will be nurtured to fruition, just as the ovum rejects many sperm, joining only with one.

Conversely the Pillar of Mercy usually affects the right side of the body, considered the masculine side. In the way of Kabbalah, the Pillar of Mercy is a path of submission to a force greater than ego. This force may be embodied as a guru, a spiritual or secular institution (the Church, the military) or a Twelve Step recovery program, to cite a few examples. How does this process of submission relate to the masculine principle? Many earth cultures believe that it is the father's function to teach a reverence for the mysteries of life. The true spiritual warrior, embodied as male or female, submits Self to a cause, an ideal or a Higher Power and allows it to work through the personality each moment. The spiritual warrior makes a commitment to explore and serve the unknowable, something greater than the human self. He or she accomplishes this through Appreciation of all that is beautiful and eternal, while cultivating the expansion of consciousness (Mercy) necessary to reach the point of "What you can conceive, you can achieve" (Impulse to Create).

The Middle Pillar is the way of balance, or direct mystical knowledge. The mystic uses the physical plane (Manifestation), Imagination and Soul Essence to cultivate the qualities necessary to experience God directly (Unity) without aid from outside intermediaries. Therefore the mystic is flexible, sometimes using the powers of the magician, sometimes submitting to a power greater than the self. The mystic makes a commitment to use both severity and mercy, as appropriate. Although so-called psychic powers may be used when necessary, there is no attachment to glory.

Living a heart-centered life in essence, the mystic is able to mediate between Divine Unity and its many manifestations in the world. Only one sphere of the Middle Pillar, Unity, represents a divine characteristic. The other two pillars have two divine spheres each— Impulse to Create and Mercy on the Pillar of Mercy, and Womb and Judgment on the Pillar of Severity. The mystic apprehends truth as a result of experience of God's presence in all things. This enfolding Unity is brought to bear in the mystic's personal life through his or her personal relationship to the world.

These days I and many of my friends find that our most fulfilling meditations often consist of sitting in an easychair or lying still and surrendering to the life force flowing through us. We don't have to do any particular practice or sit in any particular position for this energy to find us. I am aware that much energy-balancing takes place when I am in this state of reverie—energy balancing for me personally and for the planet. Often the energy flows through me in the form of symbols. At first different geometric forms may struggle with each other. One gains ascendancy, then the second absorbs the first. Eventually these symbolic struggles iron out my inner imbalances, and I feel peace. My goal in these meditations is to reach a state of rest in Unity where there are no desires, no power drives toward manifestation. In this state I am One With All Things.

In this book I write as a mystic sharing with other mystics. Our common belief is that the truth is knowable, that it comes to us both from within ourselves and a Higher Power, and that we can feel it through the signals provided by our bodies. From the vantage point of the Tree of Life, we as mystics use all the centers of consciousness (sephiroth).

The Lightning Flash of Reunion Meditation

I suggest that you record this technique, or as much of it as you want to practice at this time. In doing this meditation always start with your awareness at your feet, and use them as a point of reference throughout the meditation. You may see colors, or you may have a primarily kinesthetic experience. If, at any center on the Tree, your inner guidance tells you not to go on, take a deep breath and return your consciousness to your feet. Follow the natural pathway down the Tree.

> *First,* take several deep breaths. Focus your attention at your
> feet. Feel your groundedness, your connectedness to the
> earth. Create a mass of energy at your feet—you will draw
> from this as you move up the Tree of Life through your body.

When you feel ready, move your awareness up your legs and into your pelvic area of genitals and hips. This is the center of creative imagination, the impetus behind manifestation on the physical plane. Breathe into your creative center. Feel and hear the tone that underlies your physical reality. Many ideas may crowd your head, or you may feel very still. Keep breathing in a regular rhythm.

As you feel centered in your pelvic area, move the energy back down into your feet. Then move the energy up again, this time moving past the pelvic area and into your left hip. This is the rational area of your consciousness, the area of intellectual structures. Your left hip area has the wisdom to show you how to achieve the things you want. Breathe into the left hip and feel the tone of your intellectual energy.

Once you feel centered in this area, let your awareness travel back down through the pelvic area, down the legs and back into the feet. Feel the rightness of your physicality. Then shoot the energy up your legs, through the pelvic area and the left hip. Now cross over into the right hip. This is the area where your emotions form habit patterns and rituals. Our purpose here is not to change any of our habits, but to observe them. Breathe into your right hip area and observe the emotional tone of your life.

When you feel ready, send your energy back down to your feet from the right hip via the left hip, pelvic area and down the legs. When it feels appropriate, shoot the energy straight up to the middle of your chest from your feet. The chest center is the seat of your essence personality. It is what makes you fully human and uniquely yourself—your soul in flesh. Feel your essence, and be at peace.

When it feels right, ask your inner self if it is beneficial to journey farther up the Tree at this time, or if you have gone far enough for now. Breathe into your inner self's response. It will be a feeling of "Let's do more," or "We've done enough." If you have journeyed far enough, carry your consciousness down to your feet via your hips and pelvic area. Stay in your groundedness for awhile.

If your inner self is eager to move up the Tree, poise yourself for this journey by sending your energy straight down to your feet from your heart center. Then shoot your energy up through the heart and into the left shoulder. This is your area of choice—the place where you make the choices that create your life. Breathe into the left shoulder and get in touch with the choices you have already made, which have shaped you into the being you are today.

When you feel ready, let your awareness descend to your feet again. Then shoot your energy back up to the heart center, traveling past it to the left shoulder, and then across the chest to the right shoulder area. The right shoulder is the center of mercy, where you see the limitless possibilities for yourself and others. Here, all things are possible. Breathe into the feeling of expansion; be grateful for your unlimited potential.

After awhile, you may feel that it's time to journey again. Let your awareness flow back down to your feet. This time, build an extra charge of energy and use it to move your consciousness straight up from the feet past the throat area. On the Tree of Life, the throat is the birth canal between human reality and divine origins. As you breathe deeply, feel you are sloughing off your human focus, returning to the Womb, the Great Mother centered in the left side of your head. This is the first of the three aspects of divinity. Here you encounter the Void—you remember what gave you the impetus to physically incarnate. Breathe into the left side of your head and meditate on this: "What is my impetus to become physically incarnate?"

When you feel ready, breathe yourself out of the Void, across the brain and into the White Hole on the right side of the head, connected with the right brain. This is the Impulse to Create—a million and one ideas emanating out from the Source. Each idea creates a universe, physical and non-physical. You are the creator here, completely limitless. Get in touch with the root ideas that underlie your universe: Your particular way of looking at things, your particular experience of Life in all its forms. Breathe deeply.

At the appropriate moment, send your consciousness back down to your feet, grounding your awareness in your familiar physicality. Your soul exists in a body—this is appropriate now. Breathe your consciousness into your feet; build the energy there. When it feels appropriate, shoot your awareness straight up through your pelvic area, heart center, throat and on up into your crown center at the top of your head. The top of your head is the center of Unity, of the Divinity contemplating itself. Breathe into this Unity. You have no need for expression here, only being. Feel complete within yourself. You are God. You are the Source. Through your breath you now experience this wholeness, this oneness, this divinity. Say to yourself, "I am the Source." Pause.

-◄o►-

Continue to experience your wholeness as a unified being. At the appropriate time you will begin to feel a creative impulse stirring within you. When this happens, let the energy travel from your crown over to the right side of your head. Breathe into this creative thought. When it feels right, move your creative thought over to the Great Womb in the left side of your head, for gestation. Let the thought develop, safe in its womb.

At the appropriate time, move the energy down through the birth canal of the throat and give birth to it in your right shoulder. Now your thought is in the physical world, but it still has limitless possibilities. You will need to make choices to focus your thought, to give it form. Move your awareness over to your left shoulder when you feel ready to make these choices. Many potentials are discarded in the left shoulder area—only one line of development survives. Breathe into your choice, and empower it.

Now you have created a thought form—experience how this feels. When you feel ready, breathe this thought form down into your essence center in the middle of your chest. At this point your thought form becomes a part of your essence expression as a human being. Breathe into your chest and feel a warm glow growing there. Once again, you are focused on the Middle Pillar, the central core of your beingness. Feel your centeredness growing stronger. You are confident your power of manifestation is being used for your highest good.

As your awareness moves to your right hip, you feel appreciation for all you have been given so far. Breathe deeply, using your awareness to solidify your emotional commitment to the thought form you have created.

When you feel ready, move your attention over to your left hip. Let ideas and plans come to mind that will assist you in practical ways to achieve your desire. Suggest to yourself that you will remember these creative plans in detail, and that you will make notes and sketches of them after the meditation is over. Your mind now naturally moves in the direction of practical planning. Breathe into your left hip, and let your strategy take over.

When your plans seem solid enough, move your attention into your pelvic area. This is the realm where thoughts and feelings balance to become personal reality—reality that we inhabit during sleep, channeling, daydreaming and sex.

Here we experience the contents of our psychic envelope. Take your time with this exercise—let the Muse come upon you, and open to the vividness of your creativity. Breathe into your pelvic area and use your inner senses to experience your thought form—smell it, taste it, picture it. Feel the texture of your energy structure. Allow yourself to sound a tone that describes it, either an inner tone or an outer tone. As you breathe deeply, give yourself up to the ecstasy of totally experiencing your creative reality.

Now you are ready to bring your attention back to the physical plane. You have experienced your reality in two different ways—merger with your Godself, and creating a thought form based on desire. Draw your attention down to your feet. Open your eyes and look around you. Sit up slowly and stretch.

Before you leave, ask yourself what you need to do physically at this time to bring your thought form into manifestation. Remember to make notes and sketches of strategies you got from your left hip center. Because you are totally committed to bringing your goal to fruition, you will do whatever is necessary, step by step.

The Lightning Flash of Creation Meditation

Another variation on the experience of creative descent from Unity is a meditation on the Lightning Flash of Creation as it descends the Tree of Life, using affirmations and colors as meditation tools. Once again we will take our awareness from spirit to matter, from the top of the head down to the feet. I would suggest you wait a few days after doing the Lightning Flash of Reunion Meditation, before tackling this meditation. As usual, get a friend to talk you through it, or make a recording of the text and play it back for yourself. Remember to take plenty of pauses to allow yourself to experience the instructions fully.

First, take several deep, slow breaths. Center your attention at the top of your head. You may feel the vibration of a white light there. Repeat the word *UNITY* several times, aloud or to yourself. Breathe deeply and relax, bathing yourself in a soft white light. Know that you are whole and complete, right now in this moment.

Soon you will sense a desire welling up inside you to express this wholeness in some way. Perhaps many ideas or pictures come into your mind. Allow your consciousness to travel over to the right side of your head, as you inhale deeply. Breathe in the color gray, allowing the Impulse to Create to permeate your mind. Repeat the word *FORCE* several times, noticing how it feels to you.

Let your awareness travel over to the left side of your head. As your awareness goes through your brain, you feel that you are entering the empty space of the *VOID.* Perhaps you hear a ringing sensation in your ears, or a harmonic of several distinct notes. You are immersed in blackness, but you have no fear. You sense the limitless potential of the *VOID.* You are at peace, breathing deeply. You sense the potentials of your life lying within you, as in a womb, gestating till the right time to bring them forth. When you are ready, choose one of these potentials to be brought to light. Softly repeat the word *FORM* several times.

Now continue your descent through the body. Breathe your attention down across your throat to your right shoulder. Focusing on a soft blue light, you will feel all heaviness dissipated. Your body feels expansive, it feels huge, encompassing all things. Repeat the word *MERCY* several times, feeling compassion for all beings. You begin to feel the space within you to bring forth your potential to the physical plane. Breathe out love and light to all beings in all worlds.

Soon you will feel drawn across your breastbone to your left shoulder. Here your energy becomes more focused. Center on a bright red light and experience the warmth of it through your breath. Now focus on one aspect of your life that you wish to prune or delete. Repeat this statement several times: *I AM THE JUDGE. I...AM THE JUDGE.* Let these words dissolve your problem—you are whole and complete in this moment. Breathe deeply.

As you feel drawn down into the middle of your chest, a bright golden light awaits you. Ask this light to create a space of golden crystal in your heart. Breathe into it and let yourself experience the beautiful delights of your creation. When you feel ready, ask to meet your essence counterpart, a golden being of light. Breathe into this being, your counterpart, accepting your wholeness and merging with the angelic being that you are.

Repeat several times, *I AM THAT I AM.* Breathing deeply, feel the golden light within you. You are a divine messenger, sent to the earth for its healing.

When you feel ready, breathe your full awareness down to your right hip, visualizing a bright green light there. Feel yourself immersed in the beauty of nature, allowing feelings of gratitude to wash over you with every breath you take. Acknowledge to yourself the help you have been given to arrive at this point on your journey. Repeat several times, *I AM GRATEFUL.* Direct love and caring to a loved one, showing them how much you care for them. After you've shared your love with them, breathe in a sense of peace and security.

Now cross over your abdomen to your left hip and breathe in an orange light. Remember that potential that you brought out of the void? You are ready to plan it now. Consider the details of this creative project—it is ready to take shape. Mentally experiment with the form of your project until it feels just right. Then, while breathing deeply, repeat the word *CRAFT* several times. If you wish, you may commit your plan to paper at this time. Or you could program yourself to remember your plan in detail when you come out of meditation.

When you feel ready, breathe your awareness down into your pelvic region and let a purple light enter your womb or genitals. Out of a deep purple mist, you now sense your project being executed in the physical world. Get all your senses involved—touch it, taste it, smell it, hear it, see it— just as you would like it to manifest in the outer world. Repeat the word *IMAGINE* several times. You can feel your project coming to fruition. There is a pregnant sense of fullness in your pelvic area—breathe into this fullness.

Now you can feel your energy tumbling out with each breath, reaching down to your feet and traveling into the earth. At your feet visualize the colors of earth tones—russet red, citrine yellow, olive green and black. These tones begin to take shape as your project's expression in the world. You feel fully physical and glad to be alive! You are fully participating in life. Your creative project fills you with energy. Repeat the word *MANIFEST* several times, each time feeling stronger. When you feel complete with the process, open your eyes and stretch, allowing your body to move around. Give yourself permission to take the appropriate action in the outer world which will bring your project to fruition.

—◄○►—

In this last meditation we have used the traditional colors which are found in many occult renderings of the Tree of Life. For a briefer experience of the three pillars of the Tree, use the Ethical Triangle Meditation earlier in this chapter.

With consistent use of the Tree of Life as a body template, you can program yourself to use your body as a vehicle for enlightenment. You will view your productivity as an outgrowth of your own self-awareness, and you will be able to return to your Source at will.

Here are a few words from my Healer Guide Nathan about Kabbalah:

The Tree of Life is a useful template to superimpose over the body. Through this system you can become aware of the body's natural process of creation and reunification. Do not think of endings as death, but rather as reunification with Source. Reunification is as natural a process as creation, and both are necessary for sustaining the physical plane. However, expanding your consciousness is as least as important as expanding the physical structures in your life, so that you can hold more "programs of consciousness" in your awareness. As you train your bodies to perform more functions of energy gathering, delving into what you now call the psychic realm, you not only expand your database, but also the energy pathways necessary to implement this information. The more pathways of consciousness you have access to, the more your potential creative expressions will increase.

Don't forget to keep your systems open—avoid rigidity in pathways of consciousness. You are connected to and, indeed, are a part of many universes of consciousness of which you have no inkling. Yet you maintain your integrity as a dynamic intelligence, capable of using your raw material—consciousness—to create your reality in new and exciting ways. We participate with you, and we empower you.

In the next chapter we will explore body correlations with another system of self-awareness—the chakra system.

CHAPTER EIGHT

◄○►

Systems of Energy Flow:
The Chakras

The word chakra means wheel in Sanskrit, the ancient sacred language of India. The chakra system provides a template to describe spinning centers of energy in the body, important to energy distribution and rebalancing. Awareness of the chakras can be a valuable tool in developing attunement to the Body Signals system.

We can look at the chakras as an energy paradigm which we can fit onto our bodies and adapt for different purposes. All systems which describe energy flow within our bodies are relative—they are not absolute for all individuals in all circumstances. Rather, they are blueprints that we can adjust to our own particular bodies, make use of and adapt for our own needs. When a system no longer works for us, we can discard it in order to open up our awareness to other approaches to self-knowledge.

So far in this book we have seen several examples of energy templates we can use in our bodies: The Hand Signals system, the "Yes" and "No" system, the Spirit Guide communication system and the Tree of Life. Other examples of physical energy grids include the twelve signs of medical astrology, the meridians and acupuncture points used in Oriental Medicine and the hundreds of nodal points called *nadis* in East Indian (Ayurvedic) medicine. Each of these systems has its own distinct value in developing balance and attunement to our inner and outer environments.

Kundalini and the Chakras

The traditional chakra system derived from the spiritual traditions of India is based on cultivation of a life force energy called Kundalini, which means "serpent coil" in Sanskrit. In the practice of Kundalini there are seven chakras, or wheels of energy, which exist both in the physical body and in the etheric body adjacent to it. The chakras are perceived as vortices of energy which act as bridges between the astral world of thoughts and feelings and the world of physical manifestation. Each of these energy centers has a role to play in the creation of our human reality.

The first chakra, also called the "root" or "base" chakra, is located at the perineum, between the anus and the genitals. Its function is to collect and distribute energy to focus on basic survival instincts. As the life force is channeled through it, the root chakra accesses the raw power used in creativity.

Esoteric literature usually depicts the second chakra as spinning in the lower abdomen. The Chinese call this center "T'an T'ien." It acts as a reservoir to collect energy for use as needed. Martial artists make extensive use of the second chakra to project "ch'i," or life force and to circulate it throughout the body. We usually associate the second chakra with the drive for creative expression, which includes both sexuality and prosperity. There is a strong correlation between the forefinger, which gives signals related to creativity, and the second chakra.

Sometimes the third chakra is called the "navel" chakra, but most descriptions locate it in the solar plexus just below the ribcage. This is the center of human personality or ego identity. Besides setting up procedures and habit patterns for individual expression, this chakra also connects us with our physical and psychic environments. When we make agreements or binding contracts, these create cords of energy in our solar plexus chakra. (See the description of the Relationship Point in the hand in Chapter 3.)

The fourth chakra is in the esoteric heart center, located not in the physical heart, but over the thymus gland in the middle of the chest, equivalent to Tiphereth on the Tree of Life. Many interpretations have been given for the meaning of the heart chakra. It has been called the center of compassion, the bridge between our humanity and divinity, and the center which motivates us to express our life purpose. Our physical heart, in expressing itself fully, pumps blood which enables our physical body to live. Our heart chakra, in expressing itself fully, gives meaning to our lives by connecting us to others through bonds of unconditional love which transcend limitations of time and space.

The fifth chakra is centered in the throat. It is concerned both with issues of communicating information and with honesty in sharing our true feelings. When this chakra is "open," that is, when the energy of communication is flowing freely through it, we will be conscious of our true feelings and will find ways to communicate them accurately. Self-expression is a keyword when focusing on this chakra.

The sixth chakra is located in the "third eye," the area just above the bridge of the nose in the middle of the forehead. This center provides a mental framework for the manifestation of our desires. Mental pathways in this chakra connect us to the minds of others and to thought forms existing in our psychic environment. The Catholic theologian Teilhard de Chardin (1879–1955) called this webwork the "noosphere," a kind of global aura or oversoul. More recently, the biologist Rupert Sheldrake has addressed this concept of shared psychic reality through his theories on "morphic resonance."

The seventh chakra, located at the top of the head, is known as the crown chakra. Its function is to help the psyche receive the inflow of energy or life force from the universe. We may experience the inflow as love and compassion, as inspiration or as an electrical flow into the body. The crown chakra is the center most commonly used for channeling Spirit Guides and Ascended Masters.

In many esoteric systems an eighth chakra exists, located several inches above the head. It acts as a gateway for information to come into our consciousness from the non-physical portions of our identity. Recently I have begun meditating with the ninth, tenth, eleventh and twelfth chakras, but because they do not have a physical base at this time in our species, they are outside the scope of this book. These chakras set up the preconditions for receiving Spirit into our physical lives.

Experiencing the Chakras

I remember when I first had a physical sensation of all seven chakras, sequentially, from the base up to the crown. I had been meditating with them for about six years, using a system, described later in this chapter, in which energy poured in through the crown chakra and then moved down the spine. One day I was part of a Kundalini yoga meditation, which featured both yoga postures and chanting. The principle of Kundalini is that energy enters the body at the base of the spine and then flows upwards—the opposite of what I had been practicing for six years. I was excited to encounter a new system of working with the chakras.

At the end of the practice we were lying down in sivasana (a restful pose). Someone started to rhythmically beat a large, resonant gong. I found this sound very soothing and drifted into a deep state of relaxation. All became quiet. Without warning, the gong sounded again. At this moment I felt the activation of each one of my chakras in ascending order, starting with the root chakra in my genitals and continuing all the way to the top of my head. (Because I had a serious hernia on my left side, the energy was prevented from coming in, and I felt it only on my right side.) The sensation was a very pleasant tingling in each center. There was no longer a doubt in my mind about the existence of Kundalini!

I felt that several aspects of this experience were significant. First, I had no expectation that this rush of energy would occur. The suddenness of the gong sound was the catalyst that propelled me into opening my chakras so that the sensations were tangible. Second, my experience conformed to the classic Kundalini technique of "raising the energy" from the lower centers in the body to the higher centers. Third, I felt the energy only on my right side because of a blockage on my left. This showed me that physical blockages can affect the chakra system.

The chakra system is a bridge between non-physical and physical planes of reality. Through it energy can be transferred from one dimension to another and back again, as in a circuit. One corollary of this belief, which is being explored by the New Physics, is that our imagination affects our physical reality in specific, and measurable ways.

Some meditators tend to be less visual than auditory, and so will probably not perceive chakras as many-petaled lotuses, wheels and other traditional symbols. Instead they may hear tones coming from these centers. Visually-oriented practitioners may perceive forms or points of light coming from the chakras. Feeling or kinesthetically oriented people may feel tingling and pressure sensations in the areas where the chakras are supposed to be. Whatever our mode of perception, the important thing is to allow our experience to become real, without excessive categorization. As we let go of the need to compulsively interpret our experiences, we can open up to pleasant and interesting sensations in our bodies more often.

I recommend that you not get stuck in one interpretation of your body signals. Try different systems of interpretation. When you feel sensations that don't fit into systems that you recognize, just relax and enjoy them! You may be creating your own template—the meaning will follow later.

Color and the Chakras

Color affects our emotions. Notice right now the colors of the clothing you are wearing. Breathe into one of the main colors. Notice how you feel. Are you comfortable, uncomfortable or neutral about this color? Right now just feel your response to this color, without interpretation.

You have probably been taught to think of color as a visual phenomenon, but in this book I encourage you to expand your capacity to feel color. Visually impaired people often learn to do this and become quite adept at it. With practice, you can use touch to identify color quite specifically—the difference, for example, between red and orange. You can do this by measuring, through touch, the amount of heat that the color throws off. Red, the slowest vibration that you can see with your physical eyes, is also the warmest color to the touch. Orange is the next warmest, then yellow and green, until we reach deep blues and violets which are actually cool. I encourage you to use paper squares of various colors to practice color discernment with your eyes closed until you can easily distinguish colors by touch. This sensitivity will come in handy during other exercises in this book.

In previous meditations we have used color as a tool to help establish an emotional atmosphere for a particular psychic intent. In esoteric lore the color gold is often connected to centering and wisdom. In our previous Kabbalah meditations we used gold to focus on the Tiphereth (Essence) center in the middle of the chest. This center is connected to the Essence Hand Signal Point located in the center of the palm. We used red to tune into the Geburah (Judgment) center, related to the Hand Signal for Structure, located just above the wrist on the outer hand. Light blue helps us focus on the Mercy center, connected to the hand signal for Unconditional Love found on the Mound of Venus underneath the thumb.

Color Exercises

Color is also a useful tool to establish a stronger link with the chakras. If you are visually creative you may work with the colors pink or green to establish a link between the heart chakra and the Unconditional Love Point on the hand. You might imagine an emerald green filling your chest cavity, while noticing the feelings this produces on the Mound of Venus Point on your palm. Allow yourself to **see** green emanating from the Mound of Venus beneath the thumb. Notice how this affects the emotional tone of the body signal—how do you feel about this color?

In this instance you are using color as an emotional amplifier to help your meditations become more vivid and real. When doing your own meditations use the colors that feel appropriate to you, even if they do not match the metaphysical norm. Experiment! There are many viable color/chakra correlations that you can use.

Two Systems of Energy Flow

I have worked extensively with two templates of color for the chakra system. Many of us know the rainbow system used in Kundalini practice—moving from red to violet in progression as we move up the spine. As described above, red is associated with the root chakra at the perineum; orange with the lower abdomen; yellow with the solar plexus; and green for the heart chakra in the middle of the chest. Light blue is correlated with the throat, indigo (purple-blue) with the third eye and violet with the crown. Sometimes practitioners skip indigo in favor of violet for the third eye, using white for the crown chakra.

The purpose of the rainbow system of meditation is to raise energy from the earth and open our vital life force (Kundalini, ch'i) to the earth's vitality. As we develop a firm sense of groundedness, we gradually increase our potential to open our sensitivity in the upper energy centers.

Let's use the solar plexus as an example. This chakra is often considered the focus of the personality, or ego identity. In the rainbow system of color/chakra correlation, yellow or **gold** is usually associated with the solar plexus chakra. Yellow, a traditional color of wisdom, helps the individual sort out his or her thoughts and feelings and aids the personality in establishing boundaries distinct from others. "This is me, this is **not** me." A sense of individual identity and security results.

When an individual feels secure within his or her own boundaries, then he or she can project a compassionate, balanced energy of self-acceptance through the next chakra ascending through the body, the heart center. Green, the color of centeredness and healing, is often associated with balanced energy in the heart chakra. When we know who we are, there is less danger of self-sacrifice in the name of compassion, at the expense of our own needs.

Initially I was taught a color system in the chakras that was different from that used to raise Kundalini, when I was affiliated with a study group called the Inner Peace Movement. The founder Francisco Coll taught that universal energy comes into the body through the top of the head, moves down the spine to the coccyx and then ascends up the front of the body and out the third eye. Coll's system (which I will call the crown chakra system) differs in several respects from the Kundalini rainbow system. Both systems associate the first chakra with the color red. The difference is that the crown system places the first chakra at the **top of the head**, not at the base of the base as in the Kundalini system. The second chakra in the crown system is located at the base of the spine at the coccyx—this is associated with orange, as is the lower abdominal center in the Kundalini system, which connects energetically to the coccyx.

The crown chakra system assigns the third chakra to the perineum—it associates yellow with this center. Yellow or gold reminds us to use our soul's wisdom in getting our needs met. The Kundalini rainbow system assigns red to this area of the body. The fourth chakra at the solar plexus is given the color blue, in contrast to the Kundalini system's gold or yellow. Blue is an empathic color, developing our sensitivity to our environment and the needs of others.

Green is assigned to the heart chakra in both the crown system and the Kundalini system. It is called the fifth chakra in the crown system, the fourth in the Kundalini system. Purple is correlated with the throat center, the sixth chakra in the crown system. The color purple is associated with trust, reminding us to open our throats as channels for the Spirit to speak through us. Purple is also traditional for the throat area in Tree of Life meditations of the Kabbalah. The Kundalini system uses blue for the throat chakra.

The crown system's seventh chakra is located in the third eye. The color white is used to focus one's attention on this chakra, in contrast to the Kundalini system's indigo or violet. White, a blend of all the colors of the spectrum, reminds us to create our reality with a sense of fullness, tapping into who we really are in our relations with the world.

Why are different colors assigned to chakras in the different systems? Because they are used differently in each paradigm. Meditating while using the crown chakra system gives us access to a different grid of energy from the Kundalini system. In the crown system we focus on channeling energy from the Universe, receiving it in through the top of the head. Meditation on the color red, the slowest vibration visible to us, helps the universal energy become tangible as it enters the physical body. In this system our raw material is not the energy that comes from the earth, as in Kundalini, but energy received from the non-physical portions of our multi-dimensional selves. We use red to help integrate the energy of Spirit into our bodies, becoming channels for the universal life force to move and speak through us.

Exercise: An Experience of the Crown System

This exercise will help you get in touch with your spiritual sensitivity through the chakra system. During this exercise we will invite energy to flow in through the top of the head, send it down the spine and then up the front of the body.

> *First*, breathe energy in through the top of your head. As you breathe, ask your Spirit Friends or Oversoul to send energy to you. Visualize a red light entering your crown, helping the vibrations of your Guides to become physical.

> *Next*, allow yourself to feel energy flowing down a pathway of Light, all the way down to the base of your spine. At the coccyx (tailbone) area you will sense an orange light. Let it build up into a ball of energy—at the same time, become aware of something that you truly desire on a deep level. Let yourself bask in this sense of desire as you focus your attention on the base of your spine.

When you feel ready, move your attention to the perineum, between your sphincter and your genital area. This is the area of survival and needs. Invite a golden light to appear in this area. As you focus on this light it will help you clarify what you really need in your life at this time. Merge with the golden light, confident that all your needs are taken care of by the universal flow.

Now let the energy flow up to your solar plexus, just below the ribcage. Breathe in a deep blue light of empathy and compassion. As you breathe you become aware of a deep empathy for all living creatures. You feel connected with your environment. Let the deep blue light build, creating a ball of energy within your solar plexus. Now you are ready to do a kind of World Peace Meditation. Breathe in your environment, feeling the peaceful blue light as it fills your stomach area. Exhale this sense of peace back into the environment. Breathe in World, breathe out Peace.

When the energy feels like it wants to move again, breathe it up to the heart center in the middle of your chest. Imagine a green ray of light, filling your heart center. Then emanate this light out from your heart center to the world. Through this green ray you are in touch with your life purpose. You are filled with balance and with a drive for self-expression as you breathe in and out.

Now allow this energy to move up to the throat center, changing to a particular shade of violet that feels right to you. As you exhale, feel that you are speaking your truth. What would you like to say? Let yourself speak your truth aloud. You are channeling your self-expression to the world around you.

When it feels right, allow the energy to move up to your third eye in the middle of the forehead, just above your brow.

Sense it as an emanation of white light. As you breathe deeply, repeat this affirmation: *I AM THAT I AM. I AM THAT I AM*. Get a sense of the power flowing out of your third eye, helping to create the reality that you know. Visualize a white light streaming out from your forehead. You are cooperating with the Divine Plan for your life.

Now return your awareness to your crown chakra at the top of your forehead. As you inhale, feel the energy of your Soul flowing into the top of your head and down to the base of your spine. As you begin to exhale the energy flows upward, up through your pelvic area...solar plexus...heart center...throat...and third eye...returning to the crown center to complete the circuit. Practice sending the energy down your spine and up the front of your body, using your breath to create a pace that is right for you. Inhale down the back, exhale up the front of the body.

When you feel complete, finish this exercise by sending a white light out your forehead. Then smooth out your energy with your hands, stroking your aura. Start at the top of your head and gently move down to your feet. Stroke both the front of the body and the back. Then stretch.

The Solar Plexus System

There are many ways that energy flows through the body. I personally have worked with the chakras in three different systems: The crown chakra system, the Kundalini system and the solar plexus system. The solar plexus has its own system of energy cords which send information back and forth from the individual to the environment and back again. Parapsychologists such as Jack Schwarz and Anthony Robbins use the solar plexus energy system in their work. They are developing conscious control of the functions of the autonomic nervous system, resulting in phenomena such as firewalking, creating and healing flesh wounds with mind power and telekinesis (causing objects to move or bend at a distance).

Human control over the nervous system while in trance is quite common during group rituals in Indonesia, India and many other traditional cultures where the people are more integrated with their earth environment. In the four-part television series *Ring of Fire*, adventurers Lawrence and Lorne Blair recount how Indonesians go into trance, pierce themselves with knives, sew up their lips and eat glass—much to the consternation of the Western tourists watching them! The Indonesians do not suffer bodily harm from these trance activities. They have complete control over their body's bleeding and pain responses while in trance, which is built up through movement and attention to the lower chakras.

Jack Schwarz has developed his own color scheme for the chakras: Red-orange for the root center; pink for the lower abdomen; green for the solar plexus (indicating that the solar plexus is his point of balance); gold for the heart; blue for the throat; indigo for the third eye and violet for the crown center.

Different energy flows exist in our bodies for different purposes. If we want to develop a sense of groundedness and solid identity, the Kundalini system would be a good tool to use. To develop sensitivity to vibrations coming from the non-physical portions of Self, the crown system would be appropriate. If we want to control the autonomic nervous system consciously while interacting with our environment, the solar plexus system would be useful. Our bodies are immensely complex energy receivers and senders—antennae, in fact! The more that we vary the frequencies of energy that we allow to flow through our bodies, the richer our life experience will be. We will tap into new and different pathways of prana (life force), encouraging our brain to use more than the "normal" 10% of its capacity.

Chakras and Sound Mantras

Just as we can use color to help energy flow through the body, so also we can use directed sound. The conscious use of color promotes clarity and empathy—the ability to "see yourself in another person's shoes." Sound can be channeled consciously in the form of chants or mantras designed to make our energy compact and organized, promoting personal initiative, helping us achieve our goals.

When our energy is focused through the conscious use of sound, we become like a wedge, able to fit between any obstacles to success. The power of directed sound is illustrated in the Biblical story of Joshua and the Battle of Jericho. Joshua led the Israelites in chanting as they marched around the fortified city. They set up a resonance which caused the walls to come tumbling down in response to their thoughts. Another example of the power of directed auditory thought comes from the building of the pyramids in Egypt and Mexico. Many metaphysical scholars now believe that the Egyptian and Mayan pyramids were built not with the sweat of slave labor, but rather with group chanting and telepathy, directing the energy of the life force (ch'i, prana).

We can use sound mantras or chants in conjunction with body signals to build strength in the chakras and in other energy centers in the body that we choose to focus on. The Sufi (Muslim mystic) sage Pir Vilayat Khan employs overtones to establish resonance in the different chakras. The sounding of overtones produces several harmonious sounds at once, which can reach deeply into the body to effect healing and change. Overtones also open up pathways to the brain which are usually underused. The medieval alchemists, Muslim, Jewish and Christian, used toning to achieve transformation of matter and consciousness, turning lead into gold, so to speak.

Exercise: Sounds, Mantras and Manifestation

The following exercise will provide an experience of using a sound mantra. We will use the sound "*EEEH*," pronounced with long *ee* as in "free." The purpose of this exercise is to open up the energy of your third eye, just above the bridge of the nose or in the middle of your forehead. In occult tradition this is the center of Magick—here directed thoughts become reality. It's a good idea, as usual, to record the text in your own voice or else ask a friend to take your through it.

First, take several deep breaths, relaxing on the exhalation. Then gently close your eyes.

Next, make the sound *EEEH*, holding your mouth in a forced smile. Keep your teeth nearly together in order to produce an overtone of several sounds blending together. This may produce a vibration in your teeth and mouth.

Now focus your attention above the bridge of your nose— your third eye. Begin to feel the vibration of this energy center. Notice whether it is tingly or warm or cool. Do you feel pressure here? Once again, make the sound *EEEH*. Perhaps a color comes to mind as you tone.

Next, notice which of your body signal points feel activated along with your third eye. These points may be in your hands or feet or in another part of your body.

At this point give yourself permission to visualize one of your goals coming to fruition. Continue to sound *EEEH*. Let your body become one big goosebump as you move into total harmony with your goal and your life purpose.

When you feel complete, open your eyes and stretch slowly. Take several deep breaths to ground yourself. You may want to gently massage yourself to spread your awareness to your muscles.

Other Sound/Chakra Correlations

Other correlations between sound and the chakras include "*AAAH*" for the heart center; "*OHM*" for the solar plexus and heart, and "*EW*" (like French "*u*") for the throat. When you practice these sounds, make overtones. The more you practice, the easier it will be. Producing overtones will have an immediate effect of expanding your sensitivity to the vibrations of Spirit. I encourage you to experiment with different ways of sounding the mantras, to find the style most effective for you.

While making the outer mantras, don't forget that you are in touch with your soul's vibration through the inner ringing in your ears. This is your soul's way of communicating in a way that goes deeper than words, through pure sound resonance. Ringing in the ears opens us up to a wider range of frequencies so that we can be more responsive to our soul's ways of working through our daily life and environment. When we are playing with a wider range of possibilities we have more room to follow our impulses and to listen to the "still small voice." Relaxation is the key to greater awareness of the inner senses.

This chapter has shown how the chakra system may be used in conjunction with color and sound to increase our sensitivity to the energy flow in our bodies. The chakra system is a template, one among many, that we can use in our bodies to expand our capacity to receive and channel the life force consciously.

CHAPTER NINE

◄O►

Creating Your Personal
System of Body Signals

Our bodies are both receivers and transmitters of information. The human body is built according to an intricate template, yet each individual chooses to develop in a unique way, expressing a distinct sensitivity. Each practitioner of Body Signals has many options for developing his or her personal system. The following suggestions may prove helpful.

> *Notice* the patterns in your body that you feel the most consistently. If you feel only one point buzzing on one hand, you still have a powerful tool for self-divination that you were not aware of before!

While meditating, send a mental picture of the grid of hand signals to your hands, one at a time. When you begin to feel a buzzing in at least one hand point, you have made contact with the Body Signals system. Now your challenge will be to learn to live in a relaxed way so that the system can work in your life.

Experiment with the chakra system. Allow energy to flow through your body in at least two different ways (see Chapter 8). First, feel life energy coming in through the top of your head, moving down your spine and into the earth. Second, feel the energy rising up from the earth to fill-your pelvic region, then moving **up** the spine and finally going out through the top of your head. As you practice these two ways of moving energy through your body, you will feel more sensitized to Spirit when using the crown chakra system. When you are practicing with the Kundalini system, you will feel more energized with earth energy. Your resulting experience will be one of inner strength and balance.

Literally walk on the earth frequently, letting your energy flow down into the earth and feeling the flow of energy from the earth in return. Creating energy exchange with the earth keeps you from getting stuck in your intellect as you begin working with new conceptual models.

Practice using the motion of your arm to get simple answers from your unconscious: Yes, no and neutral. Experiment with asking different aspects of Self about the same question. You might ask both your Guides, your inner child and your higher self, "Is this a good year for me to buy a new car?" "A different car?" "How about next year?" Each part of your extended psyche will provide a slightly different perspective on your intended action, which will contribute a richness to your decision-making process.

Clear your communication channels with each part of your psyche by asking a blanket question, such as, "Guides (inner child, higher self, inner male, inner female), are you willing to answer a question for me at this time?" If your Guides' answer is "no," maybe it's more appropriate for another part of you to deal with the issue. You can also ask questions of the feeling nature of objects in your environment—plants, animals, furniture, power objects. "Plant, would you like to move to a different window?"

Sometimes you will not get clear answers from **any** portion of your consciousness. This may be an indication to drop the process of questioning and just trust your gut feeling. If you are tense or tired, you may need to let go and relax before questioning further. It is important to feel a sense of inner clarity while you are engaged in the questioning process. Otherwise you easily may manufacture the answers you want.

When you feel a sense of fatigue after asking your unconscious for several answers, it may be a sign that your inner child is tired of answering "head questions." Perhaps you are trying to put too many limits on your instinctual inner knowing. You may need to expand your focus by asking questions from a heart perspective, from your inner feelings, while de-emphasizing the conceptual component of your questioning. Let your thoughts and feelings come into balance to give you the insights that you need.

While meditating, open yourself up to receive chills and goosebumps from your Spirit Guides. When you feel goosebumps on a certain part of your body, such as your neck, use the "yes" and "no" system to ask, "Is this tingling a signal from one of my Guides?" If the answer is "yes" you can be more specific: "Spirit Guide, do you prefer a male identification? A female identification? Neither?" "Are you one of my personal team of Guides? Are you here on a special project?" "Have I known you when you had a physical body?" And so on. Along with "yes" and "no" answers to these questions you may receive a verbal message, a tangible feeling or a picture that flashes through your mind. Use the "yes" and "no" technique as a springboard to unlock your own sensitivity.

Vary the forms of your communication with aspects of your inner self. **Write** a message from your Spirit Guides. **Draw** the message from your inner child. **Speak** the words of wisdom coming from your higher self. **Move your body** creatively in response to your inner male or female.

Checking In with Body Signals

Each of us develops our own mechanisms to keep us on track and warn us when we are deviating from our life purpose. As we work with our body signals consistently, we will develop our own physical code based on our own version of energy flow. Prana (life force) flows through many physical systems—our blood, nerves, lymph, skeletal structure and muscles, to name a few.

My body has developed a personal warning signal in the form of blood flowing from my right nostril—never my left. This attention-getter occurs occasionally when I am trying to suppress acknowledgment of my real needs. This body signal seems more easily activated when I've drunk caffeinated coffee, but in itself caffeine is not the trigger. Black tea does not have the same effect.

I recall the first time I experienced the "bloody nose" body signal. It was during a quiet meditation in my Amsterdam hotel room. I had cut my ties to my hometown of Chicago and had traveled for several months in Europe, seeking a possible relocation site. At this point in Holland I no longer felt bonded to Chicago, yet I sensed the need to return to the United States. During the meditation I scanned North

America and saw a bright golden light over Santa Fe, New Mexico. I had visited Santa Fe before and had felt comfortable there. I thought, "This is a place where it would be compatible for me to live."

My inner critic retorted, "Santa Fe is not practical. How could you make a living there?" The next thing I knew, my right nostril was bleeding profusely. There was no external reason for this—I had been lying down peacefully—so I asked my inner self what the bloody nose meant. In reply, I got the distinct feeling that the blood flow was a kinesthetic response to the pressure of denying my true feelings. It got my attention sufficiently so that when I returned to the United States I packed my things and drove to Santa Fe for a nice long respite which was spiritually productive. I was able to further my work on citizen diplomacy to the former Soviet Union and prepare for another journey there. My body signal of the bloody nose had been warning me not to suppress my true feeling as it came up to consciousness during meditation.

Why blood flow from the right nostril and not the left? Perhaps the capillaries on the right side of my face are more fragile. It also could be that because the right side of the body is generally the **outflow** side, the blood flows in response to blocked impulses—blood, instead of creativity.

Physical Astrology

Knowledge of correlation between the body and the astrological signs may be useful in enhancing one's relationship to body signals. Aries traditionally rules the head; Taurus, the neck and throat; Gemini, the nervous system, the arms and lungs. Cancer is concerned with digestion in the stomach; Leo rules the heart and upper back. Virgo rules the intestines; Libra, the kidneys and the small of the back; Scorpio, the reproductive system and the organs of elimination. Sagittarius rules the pelvic girdle and the thighs; Capricorn, the knees; Aquarius, the calves and ankles and Pisces, the feet.

Each of the signs is symbolic of a certain quality in the human personality. Aries is connected with originality, impulsiveness and new beginnings; Taurus, with stability and comfort; Gemini, with communication. Cancer is the mother figure of the Zodiac, with a strong sense of place and family. Leo is the leader that calls attention to itself. Virgo organizes details and puts them into order. Libra is concerned with balance and harmony in all its relationships. Scorpio is the transformer, either through pain or pleasure. Sagittarius is the philosopher and explorer or traveler. Capricorn rules ambition and persistence; it takes care of its own. Aquarius is the idealist who serves the collective; often it is more comfortable with social groups than with intimacy. Pisces is the mystic which explores the vast sea of the unconscious.

From the Body Signals perspective we see that the feet would mean something much different in the context of astrology than in the Tree of Life. Once again, we learn to fit several templates of consciousness over the physical body, and to interpret signals from the unconscious in the context of the particular paradigm we are working with—each paradigm has its own ground rules.

Pain and Illness as Messages

Users of the Body Signals system learn not to judge the body when it produces pain and illness. Usually the physical reason for the imbalance becomes apparent later, once we have grasped the lesson that the symptoms were meant to teach.

I remember one incident which underscored the psychic nature of illness to me. I picked up a chest cold as a result of a confrontation with a friend in which he psychically attacked me out of jealousy. This was done covertly, with a mask of goodwill, so that for two weeks I suffered without knowing why I had gotten the cold and without being able to get rid of it. I tried every holistic method I could think of: Acupuncture, moxibustion, aromatic oils. Although these methods provided temporary relief, the cold kept returning.

Finally I visited a scale model of the Great Pyramid and was meditating there with some friends. When I addressed the issue of my cold, my inner voice said, "Stop trying to get rid of this cold; you're not ready yet!" I received the distinct impression that I was carrying my friend's negativity, and that the best course of action would be to confront him directly and return his energy to him. In this way

I would be free both of the psychic attack energy and the cold. I decided to do this without delay.

At my next meeting with my friend I asked for the courage to be honest with him in a loving way. My intent was to help him take responsibility for his actions by acknowledging the truth of my own perceptions. By the end of our conversation I felt completely clear, but my friend had cold symptoms!

This incident helped me and my friend to grow in self-awareness, despite the discomfort involved. I learned a lesson that it's difficult to release illness when that energy comes from someone else and I have unconsciously accepted it as my own. Otherwise my experience is that healing is spontaneous when I am dealing with my own issues or letting go of someone else's problems consciously.

Each of us will find that our body has its own unique ways of capturing our attention, both pleasantly and unpleasantly. It may be through unconscious signals over which we have no control—an itching in the nose, a twitch in the hand, a sudden pain in the shoulder, a feeling of lightheadedness. As we realize that every experience in life can be valuable, we will not blame the body for giving us uncomfortable feelings or signals that we do not understand immediately. We will not sedate the body with drugs so that we cannot feel what it is trying to tell us. Instead we will learn to pay attention to how the body mirrors our thoughts and feelings. viewing the body as a mirror rather than as an enemy, we can leave past hurts and illnesses behind once the lesson has been learned. Instead of treating disease as an unshakable reality, we can focus on how to support and heal all of our many bodies, physical and non-physical, in the present moment.

Exercise: Taking the Edge Off Discomfort

Often through therapy or meditation we arrive at a deep level of truth about our fears, but still remain in discomfort, emotionally or physically, about these issues. We may feel enmeshed in the pattern of our habits and addictions, without clear replacement patterns in sight. In these situations we can use the power of visualization to take the edge off our uncomfortable feelings, removing the sense of panic from our emotional body so that we can find enjoyment in the present moment.

Let's try a brief visualization now.

Imagine the color blue, an ice blue, cool and soothing. See this color flowing into an area of your body where you feel pain or constriction. Breathe into this area and ask your body if it will allow itself to be comforted. You may want to touch or hold yourself in this area, sending love through your body.

As you relax, you may receive thoughts and feelings from your unconscious. These may or may not seem connected to your body sensations. Send love and light to these thoughts and feelings, knowing that on some level they are mirroring what you are experiencing in your body.

Remember that you deserve love in every situation, no matter what the circumstances. Keep inhaling love in the form of ice blue light until you feel yourself letting go of tension and pain. You are permeated by love and light.

In doing the above exercise you are not denying your feelings or trying to repress the pain signal that your body is sending you. You are not ignoring the message that the discomfort holds for you. You are remembering to nurture yourself in the midst of a difficult situation.

My Spirit Guide Betty says:

Why not try, every day, to listen consciously to what your body is trying to tell you? Take a deep breath and relax into a comfortable position. Begin to talk to your body by asking it questions coming from the heart. You might ask your right arm, Do you feel balanced?" "Is there a part of you that is holding more stress than other parts?" "What can I do to support you?"

*Get to know your body's functioning patterns. Find out how the human liver handles the body's toxins. Then use this information to help you tune in psychically to the functioning of **your own** liver. Every person has created his or her own universe, with its own laws of creation and destruction. Anatomical information can provide you with a useful framework for learning how to work with your body intuitively.*

*Most of all, expect surprises from your body. Thus far you know very little about your body's true capabilities. The peoples of Indonesia who eat glass, walk on fire and pierce their bodies with sharp objects, all without ill effects, are illustrating a very important point to your species—that the body exists **for your convenience** and **for your learning experience**. Once you learn to treat your body as a communication system with your inner self, you will lose your fear of it and will be able to tap its hidden abilities.*

In the same vein, my higher self (called Chan) says:

Balance is most important. Bless your fears. Balance does not mean that you live in perfect harmony at all times. Balance is the commitment to yourself so that you will pick yourself up when you fall, and right yourself. To do that, you must have commitment to balance.

When you feel depressed about your lack of progress, learn to go to the hidden places in your psyche that feel cut off from the Whole and gently caress them. Make them feel welcome, for they too have a message to share with your soul. In your merger with crystals, trees and grass, do not forget to merge with neglected parts of yourself. In this way you will know peace and through you, society will know it.

Developing our Intuition

Intuition is related to empathy—we must become "the other" to acti-vate our inner knowing. As we link up with other beings intuitively, we lose our sense of separateness and feel connected to Essence. Intu-ition is a kind of radar that senses when energy patterns are approach-ing our field of concern. The breadth and depth of our field of concern is up to us. We could become aware of world events before they hap-pen or while they occur. We could extend our radar into our personal future or the probable future of our loved ones. We could use intuition to see the past in a different light. I consider intuition to be an aspect of instinct, a bridge between the physical and non-physical portions of our awareness. In developing consciousness of body signals, we activate both our physical and auric knowing and integrate it as physicalized intuition.

Our intuitive side is constantly processing more data than our conscious minds can comfortably hold in a particular moment. That is why often we do not understand why we know the things we know. It takes the linear portions of the conscious mind some time to catch up with the perceptions of the inner knowing. However, as we live committed to our intuitive truth, life situations will provide ample confirmations of our hunches.

When we remember that the true nature of time is simultaneous, that from the Oversoul's perspective all events are happening at once, we can understand the connected nature of the disparate themes in our lives. We will see that our life forms a coherent webwork, a pattern of *leitmotifs* which are linked by the common theme of learning experience. As we learn to let go of the tyranny of linear thought, we will become more open to the multi-tiered aspect of moment-to-moment reality.

Our intuition exists for our convenience, to make our life richer, smoother and more fun! During the periods when I was short of money, I would often feel a buzzing on my hand when a thought about finding a bargain came into my head. I remember following an impulse to visit a record store and finding a good but inexpensive recording of a piece I had wanted for a long time. My intuition still gives me nudges to go shopping at stores which turn out to have sales on the things I want!

Body Signal Support Groups

In addition to your personal work to develop physical intuition, it may be beneficial to join your efforts with others of like mind. It is important to create a favorable atmosphere for expansion of consciousness if your ego is to feel safe in letting go of control over your body's perceptions. It may feel less daunting to explore new functions of the body if you are part of a cadre of trusted friends with whom you can feel safe. A harmonious group can create a unified energy field so that experimentation in body awareness can be carried out at an accelerated yet smooth pace.

Here are some suggestions for group work:

- If your goal is to bond with other group members, a group of six to eight is ideal. It provides group power without sacrificing intimacy. If you prefer to develop your sensitivity in your own way, but under the safety of a group umbrella, a larger group may work just as well for you.

- Begin your group meeting with a quiet time, followed by some form of group attunement—chanting, centering the aura, visualization.

- Call in the Spirit Guides of the group members to assist you all in developing your sensitivity. Allow yourselves to **feel** these Guides on your bodies at consistent spots.

- During each session develop a theme which relates to a Body Signal hand point. For instance, do a session on feeling truth resonating in the body and correlate it with the truth finger (little finger).

- Engage in a group mediation to consciously bring in the template of Body Signals to your aura, that is, to the energy grid surrounding you. If you feel resistance during this process, acknowledge this fact: Acknowledgment enables you to let go of the fear and breathe into the love that is really there.

- Allocate time in which group members can channel messages for themselves and for each other. While these messages are being delivered, both the channel and other group members will probably feel spontaneous body signals which will confirm or revise what is being said. This is a good system of feedback for budding channelers.

- Before closing the meeting, use the group energy to send healing vibrations to the planet and the universe, including all forms in your quickening of consciousness.

- Take your expanded sensitivity home to practice with between meetings!

Body Signals as a Lifestyle

As we discussed in Chapter 7, body signal sensitivity helps us travel the path of the mystic. This means we accept a direct connection between ourselves and the truth of our Source, whether we work with such intermediaries as Spirit Guides or not. When we accept that our inner truth manifests outwardly in our lives, we set up preconditions for body signal perception. Then we can regard the buzzing in our truth finger as a normal confirmation of a thought we've just had. When our healing finger buzzes, confirming ideas about diet that a friend is sharing, we accept it as a part of life, not an unusual phenomenon.

Many years ago, before I embarked on a program to develop my sensitivity consciously, I accepted that my intuition would save me in times of crisis. I would rely on it heavily at those times. Now that I accept that intuitive sensibility is an everyday part of life, I do not need a dramatic situation to activate it. Ironically, I am more comfortable with being in a physical body, now that I understand that the physical plane is not a prison of limitations. Body signals help me to stay connected to my greater reality while making my daily choices. This is important for me as a mystic—it helps me integrate both the physical and the trans-physical aspects of Self. Now that I no longer see the body as cut off from Spirit, I can relax and have a good time!

This chapter closes with a series of messages from Guides and transpersonal aspects of self. I suggest that you use these messages to get ideas for your own personal transformation.

Message from the Teacher Paul

About groupwork: Convene periodically with trusted friends to create the kind of reality you want. Do it as an exercise for the evening, not seriously, but in play. Surrender your conscious agenda to the group energy as a whole. Let it lead you to a group consciousness that will empower you, while at the same time providing you with a framework for growth. This can be done in small groups or in large ones—it makes no difference where the energy of the group is concerned, only from the point of intimacy between participants.

Sustained growth occurs in the collective. You are all part of the same Mystical Body, so why not share this energy with each other.

I am Paul, part of the collective whole which is the Christ consciousness.

Message from Ariana, Goddess of Truth

Encouragement from within is always important. Look to see how each of you has empowered yourselves in your lives. When you find an area that seems to make sense to you, explore it, cultivate it and, finally, live it. By this we mean the area of consciousness that turns on a light for you within. Each person has a specific area, or vibration, that he or she chooses to inhabit. This differentiation comes from Essence—you are all different, though each of you has a role to play in the Whole.

We would suggest this conceptual framework at this time: Understand your wholeness, live your truth, share with others. That is enough. We come to guide you frequently, with groups and without. We are with you. Your entity rejoices in your wholeness. Be at peace.

Message from the Spirit Guide, Seth

Now, in this period of expansion for your species, you are ready to receive messages from other life forms—dolphins and whales, for example. They tell you that you are polluting their environment to the point where it will be imperative that they leave— to find another environment where they can grow comfortably and with ease. This concept of growing in comfort and ease is most important to your species right now. It is essential for you all to recapture the spirit of ease and fun if you are to survive and have a future on this planet.

*The scramble for wealth and power is the undoing of your species. You have been told this for millennia, but the time has come when you can no longer **afford** to play these games. Your planet's viability for your species is in question right now. Your species will survive, in all probability, but the quality of life may not be high. Do you want your children and your children's children to live in such a world?*

We repeat: Start taking responsibility for your actions, down to the smallest detail. Do not serve the collective at the expense of yourself, but be a mutual beneficiary. Make sure that everything you do fits in with your life purpose, whether it is work or play— you do not have time to engage in off-track activities. We do not say that your activities must serve someone else's concept of God *or truth—they must serve **you**, in your essence. Let all other activities go. Ask yourself, "Does this serve me in my life purpose?" and then follow your heart.*

We go into the Light now, to merge with our friends.

Message from My Higher Self Chan

Topic: Energy structures. What you seek, you have inside you. That is the point of this book. You create energy structures for your own purposes, quite unconsciously sometimes. When confronting an energy structure stronger than your own, you may choose to give in, to go with the flow or you might create an alternate structure that serves you better. Since you do not always know what you are doing, or feel that you have a choice, it may be difficult to create your own reality the way you want it.

When an energy structure serves you, you have a tendency to cultivate it, to strengthen it through use. When it no longer serves you, discard it. It can be dissolved and the resultant energy used to create something new. It is not useful to maintain too many energy structures that you feel responsible for, long after they have ceased to serve you. It is better to move on and create other support structures in different contexts. What you see as "location," we view as "context." That is why seemingly different situations may reflect the same context, and why a person's experience of the two situations may be quite similar.

For example: A husband and wife divorce; the wife immediately becomes involved with another man and marries him. She does not dissolve the emotional support structure of her first marriage, and so the second relationship has much the same dynamic as the first. Her new husband may find it too much work to disband the energy structures from his previous relationships as well. Therefore the new couple are living out their pasts with each other, probably unconsciously. They are not insisting that the rules of the new relationship be changed to suit their present needs.

In each relationship there are unspoken rules, holdovers from the previous relationships of the participants, whether these occurred in the present life or in previous incarnations. It is important to see the implicit rules as conveniences designed to facilitate the current relationship, not as a theory to be obeyed in all circumstances. Rules are not truths.

In society you have carried over many customs and traditions both from your ancestors and from other societies. Sometimes the mass grouping reincarnates together with little evolution of consciousness—so the same lessons continue. We believe that the ancient Romans have become the modern day Americans. Both societies have a lesson about public moral posturing versus private decadence. But because of improved communications systems, it is harder to fool yourselves now in modern America. You are left with the conclusion, "BE YOURSELF." That seems to be the most important lesson facing America today.

For the human race, I would say that it is acceleration of consciousness which is most important right now—the realization of how quickly thoughts create reality. Computer games, where the participant is encouraged to see himself in one harrowing scenario after another, provide a good example of the power of choice to change circumstances immediately. People are moving around the globe without feeling that they must give up their identities and traditions in the process. The "melting pot" ideal is slipping away in the United States, to be replaced by the "mosaic," perhaps. A sense of national identity, of being an "American," is no longer strong enough to carry the weight of personal growth. In the Global Village we are all one, yet each is responsible for his or her own identity.

Let us consider the differing destinies of the former Soviet Union and the United States. These two empires recently commanded the loyalty of the majority of the earth's inhabitants. Each was founded on visionary ideals. In the United States, individual liberty was planned to be paramount; in the Soviet Union the rights of the collective were placed above those of the individual. National structures evolved out of these ideals, but inevitably the ideals eroded and cynicism set in. A society may attempt to return to its original ideals and to re-inspire its people, giving them a new sense of purpose and direction. America is attempting to do this with its rhetoric of 'family values.' The Soviet Union tried it with 'glasnost' and 'perestroika.' But if the ideals are not sufficiently powerful to motivate the mass consciousness, then the society falls and its national structures dissolve. This has been the case in the former Soviet Union.

In the United States people perceive a widespread dissolution of the **personal** *fabric of life. Traditional emotional support structures such as the nuclear family are in decline. Calls to revive them are not really motivating people to change their behavior. A moral vacuum results. We suggest that the vacuum can be filled with a personal commitment to greater conscious awareness. The physical body is a given, and is therefore a good place to start on this quest. Commitment to greater sensitivity in your own body will lead to greater connectedness between individuals, as each person has a clearer sense of his or her own energy field—where it begins and ends, what its needs are, and how it interfaces with others.*

During transition periods one energy structure often feels superimposed on another—the future and the past both converging on the present. Even new people in your life may respond to you in old ways, because you each are still enmeshed in outmoded energy structures. Therefore it is important to seek validation during transition times, either from those who are also making transitions, or from people who are already where you want to be. From the point of view of energy, getting support from your Future Self and its friends is the most creative interface possible—through meditation you contact the self you have the potential to become. This creates results very quickly. In a relationship, previously established energy structures (habits, boundaries, rules) are a good source of raw material to build on, whether both parties have actively created them or not. Communicate what you want!

If one partner is using the Body Signals system consistently and the other wants to expand rapport with him or her, they could adopt the Body Signals system as a bridge of communication. For example, they could use the Telepathy Point in the hand to establish mental channels for communication. After awhile, they could use the Communication Point on the wrist to create astral thought forms that would enhance the growth of their relationship.

Create your own private code, as lovers and friends have done through the ages. By using Body Signals in this way, you will enhance your psychic sensitivity at the same time as you validate your perceptions through the emotional support of a relationship!

CHAPTER TEN

--<o>--

Beliefs as a Framework
for Healing

How alienated are you from your environment? Do you mistrust plants and animals until they prove themselves? Is the weather your enemy? Are you physically comfortable only within a narrow band of temperature extending no more than ten degrees?

Do you view your body with fear and dread, wondering what new pain or discomfort it plans to inflict on you? Are you suspicious of people at first meeting? Do you frequently catch yourself thinking or commenting about the uncertainty and unfairness of life?

An affirmation to counter suspicion: **I live in a safe universe**. (*cf. The Nature of Personal Reality* by Jane Roberts) **The world is my playroom. I choose to learn my lessons with gentleness and fairness.**

Affirmations are positive statements of inner truth. We can use affirmations in two ways: Receptively, as an internal response to bring in more Light, whether our outer circumstances are pleasant or not; and creatively, as building blocks for a personal belief system that we make by choice, not acquire by inheritance. Each of us has the right to create a belief system tailored for our own life lessons.

I suggest that you create a belief system which makes room for the body as a receiver and a sender of psychic impressions. The following affirmation may help: **My body provides me with the answers I need to steer my course in life effectively.** The following prayer may also be useful: **I ask for clarity in interpreting the signals my body sends me.**

Affirmations are designed to support the development of your inner belief system. Like prayer, they provide a conscious link to a Higher Power. Sometimes it is important to clear away negative, destructive energies before positive affirmations can be effective. We can make **negation** statements, conscious denials of the illusion in which we find ourselves. Negation can clear our energy field of limiting habit patterns and thought forms. Conscious negation disempowers aspects of our reality that no longer serve us. The effect is much different from unconscious denial which, being based on fear, keeps us stuck in old patterns, afraid to directly confront the reality we have made for ourselves. One useful negation from *A Course in Miracles* goes like this: **Nothing I see means anything.**

When we confront our reality and find it lacking, we can respond in a variety of ways. By fixating on the problem, we may build up our discomfort to such an extent that we motivate ourselves to change our circumstances. We may also live out the maxim: "When life hands you a lemon, make lemonade." In doing this we use our present surroundings as a springboard to our goal.

The physical plane experience is a dynamic tension between seemingly immutable circumstances and creative goals which transcend them. It is important to consciously acknowledge that the permanence of circumstances is illusion. If we stop to look at our own life history, we will find many instances of sudden change—decisions thrust upon us, perhaps, which changed the quality of our lives irrevocably.

Robert Fritz addresses the issue of problem-solving extensively in his marvelous book, *The Path of Least Resistance*. My understanding of his premise is that by goal-setting we can create a set of favorable circumstances that will further the development of our Essence. Often what we have thought of as the path of least resistance is actually inertia or non-action. Our habits have kept us bound to situations we no longer want. It actually takes a greater amount of physical and psychic energy to resist a change that is ready to happen as a result of our natural evolution, than it does to just surrender to the flow of our growth.

Feelings of obligation, powerlessness and inertia give rise to circumstance-centered behavior. We may think, "I have no choice about seeing my relatives—it's _____ (Christmas, Passover, Thanksgiving, etc.)." Feeling compelled to resign oneself to unsatisfactory circumstances is a form of giving away power. "Of course I can't live my own life and do what I want—I have obligations. I'm married; I have children."

In these situations we have forgotten that circumstances wither and die when no one gives them power. We may be afraid of drawing our attention away from what exists, because we will have to enter the Void to create something new. Our fear of the unknown tells us that the new thing may be even worse than what we have now. Our challenge is to be honest with ourselves, so that we create our joy from a very deep level in our consciousness.

Beliefs and Body Signals

Body signals remind us of our true feelings. We may start to tell a friend, "Sure, I'd love to go to the movies with you tonight." Then we feel a constricting pain in our little finger, the truth finger. We amend, "On second thought, I'm really tired. What I really want to do is stay home and rest." Our truth finger starts buzzing pleasurably. We've just saved ourselves from a tedious evening.

In the course of our random thoughts, our body signals will give us confirmation when we hit upon a thought that would be good to pursue. A creative project, perhaps; or a fantasy that could become a reality with proper empowerment. "If I really had a choice, I'd build

my own house." Our forefinger, connected to creativity and abundance, starts to tingle. "Maybe it really is possible!" Creative ideas start racing through us, illustrating how this project might be accomplished.

My body signals always let me know when I encounter my highest good. My body signals remind me of the truth about myself. Self-delusion dissolves in the presence of my body signals.

Shifting Gears with Body Signals

The more systems we use in getting to know our bodies, the better. Each system accesses a piece of the puzzle but not all of it. Astrological correlation may work well for one Body Signals practitioner; another may start to embody the Kabbalistic Tree of Life; a third may experiment with several directions of energy flow through the chakras. Eventually all three may become comfortable with all available systems of energy flow through the body.

We can use the body as a flexible tool that can contain many distinct vibrations and perspectives of truth. One vibration of truth does not cancel out another. As we allow ourselves to shift gears to experience truth physically, the body becomes a clearinghouse to process both external data, internal information and trans-personal messages.

It is useful to be consistently aware of our body throughout the day. When we cannot feel the energy coursing through our body, flowing up and down the spine, for example, we can take the time to get centered. We could energize our energy field (aura) with our hands, or do a deep breathing exercise, or visualize a color flowing into the body from the earth or the universe. As long as we feel energy in our body, we have raw material to create with and accompanying signals to interpret.

The philosopher Gurdjieff spoke of developing different centers of consciousness in the process of one's human evolution. More recently, the *Michael Teaching* has presented this perspective on growth (*cf. Messages from Michael* by Chelsea Quinn Yarbro). According to Michael there are seven centers, vantage points from which we look at the world: Higher intellectual, intellectual, higher emotional, emotional, moving, sexual and instinctual. We may look at the instinctual center as the window through which come body signals from the non-physical parts of our psyche. The instinctual center is a neutral gear bridging the higher centers of transpersonal consciousness with the lower centers of personality.

In the context of the Body Signals system, the experience of the feelings themselves would relate to the instinctual center. The interpretation of the signals would be a function of the intellectual centers. Using the signals to relate to the surrounding world from one's inner truth would be a function of the emotional centers. Acting with self-empowerment while using one's body signals as validation would be an application of the action centers, moving and sexual. Moving center relates to stamina and endurance. Sexual center, in a spiritual sense, is the celebration of the flesh through accomplishment, and by nurturing self through interacting with life. Although most people are most comfortable coming from one vantage point, through the use of body signals we can become comfortable with all of them, moving from one center to another as appropriate.

Body Signals as a Framework for Interconnectedness

An immediate effect of using the Body Signals system will be an increased sense of connectedness to the world around us. This will help slay the dragon of separation which has plagued the West for the last three thousand years since the advent of patriarchy. Our goal is not the restoration of matriarchy, but rather the creation of new social structures based on **balance** and **free flow of energy**. As we regularly experience body signals, it will be difficult to pretend that we are closed universes unto ourselves. "There are no closed systems" (*cf. Seth Speaks* by Jane Roberts). As we receive messages from different portions of self, we will be more open to the truth around us. We will understand that truth is not limited to so-called sentient beings, much less to the human race. Every molecule is alive—every atom has its message to share.

The Body Signals system creates a conceptual framework in which our "paranormal" experiences can be explained, worked with and expanded upon. One difficulty with being a mystic in Western society has been the aura of secrecy surrounding mystical experiences—as children we are not encouraged to share them, but to cordon them off in the recesses of our minds and keep them hidden. Mystical experience is viewed as impractical. It is thus difficult for us Western mystics to integrate our experiences sufficiently into our working consciousness so that they provide the glue to make sense of our lives. The Body Signals system is one way to set up a resonant tone or context so that our mystical experiences make sense. Our intellectual centers can then use our intuition as a foundation to provide us with direction in life.

My experience of firewalking illustrates the importance of having a conceptual framework to integrate psychic experience. The whole evening was an energy high—I learned about energy dynamics in a group setting, about "mind over matter," and that firewalking with my friends three abreast was more fun than doing it alone! I will never forget the feeling of surrender to trance which literally pulled me to walk over the coals without being burned.

The next day, however, I felt a sense of letdown. What was I to do with this experience, how was I to apply it to my life? I filed it away with many other experiences that proved the physical body is a malleable energy system with bendable rules of operation. That weekend I was involved with a workshop on power animals in the chakras. This information had more lasting impact because I was already working with the chakra system and with power animals on a regular basis. The material expanded on an already existing framework. The firewalking experience did not, and few leads were given to help integrate it. In retrospect I am convinced that firewalking and other similar paranormal phenomena will have to be integrated into a larger conceptual framework in order to exert the maximum impact possible on the human psyche.

The implications of the Body Signals system often excite practitioners and turn their lives around. The system provides a context for tapping into the psyche's unlimited potential. Our bodies are fertile ground for experimentation with consciousness. In the Body Signals system we do not use the physical to **define** our consciousness, but rather as a springboard for personal development. This system appeals to people who recognize the fluidity of the physical plane and want to explore this aspect of their experience further.

Personal Reality and Energy Structures

As we begin to realize that what we thought of as metaphysical truths are really energy structures that we can adapt and play with, we lose our awe of the physical plane's apparent solidity. We become more willing to experiment with changing our life conditions. We use the energy structures that surround us for our own purposes, losing our residual submission to a "truth" outside ourselves.

Let's apply this principle of experimentation to the chakra system. Chakras are actually structures for energy flow from the physical to the etheric or astral and back again—from the real to the potential and vice versa. Several systems of energy flow make use of the chakra system, as we have seen in Chapter 8—Kundalini energy flows up from the earth; the circulation of ch'i begins in the lower abdomen and travels up the spine; energy for channeling flows **down** the spine and the solar plexus acts as a clearing house for interaction between the individual and the environment. Which chakra system is correct? In experimenting we learn that we may use different flows of energy for different purposes: Channeling, grounding and empathy, to name a few. As we penetrate the shroud of mystery around so-called metaphysical truth, which implies that the truth exists in the form itself and not in the intention of its use, we realize that the chakra system and other frameworks exist for our convenience, to help us grow in consciousness.

The inner child concept, as I have presented it in this book, is also an energy structure or tool rather than a bundle of traumatic memories or an immature self which must "grow up." I view the inner child as a dynamic symbolic connection to the instinctual self. Our instincts provide us with a psychological foundation for input on personal survival. Without respect for the inner child connection, the individual will be erratic in his or her growth efforts because a sense of ongoing emotional support will not be present. Without encouragement from within, the "path of least resistance" principle will operate so that the psyche will shut down to new experiences when it is feeling over-whelmed. Growth thus proceeds slowly. When fears come up, the inner child structure provides a healthy way for the individual to get in touch with those fears and just "be" with them, instead of numbing the fears with addictive or compulsive behaviors. When an individual recog-nizes that the inner child's needs come first, beyond any moral code or social pressure, a deep feeling of inner security takes root. This gives rise to true compassion and service—as we consistently give to our-selves, so we also give to others.

All of the intuitive modalities presented in this book—the Tree of Life, the arm pendulum, points of contact for Spirit Guides, physi-cal astrology and, of course, the system of hand signals—are meant to provide positive energy structures which will encourage sensitiv-ity to intuition in the body. When we get used to a sufficient number of these paradigms, we begin to perceive the body itself as an energy structure designed for our growth and learning.

The secret of a smooth-running body could be stated as follows: Make good health your goal, and do whatever is necessary to achieve it. How will you know what is necessary? Ask your body what it wants! Once you become attuned to your body through physicalized intuition, you will find it much easier to discern your real needs.

At this time, our real challenge is not to discover that the body has wisdom; rather, it is to perceive the physical plane itself as a dynamic structure ready to serve our growth.

My body exists to serve me in my growth. For this I am grate-ful. Thank you, Body!

Channeling from My Higher Self

Greetings, we are Chan. Your body is a control center for your conscious awareness. It is also, more accurately, a battery that can hold a certain amount of charge. When the battery can no longer hold the charge required for physical life, the energy goes elsewhere—this is called death.

It is not wrong to want to change focus, that is, to die, but we want you to know that the physical body is capable of carrying much more of a charge than you realize. You may recharge your physical battery on an everyday basis through meditation and concentration. Not to do this puts you as victim of your circumstances. There is still a large section of the mass consciousness on this planet which is subject to entropy, that is, to the belief in a gradual winding down or diminishment of life force channeled.

You, however, do not need to be a part of this "gloom and doom" consciousness. It is better for you to pioneer new life forms, that is, new ways of being alive. Put your focus on this, and you can then focus on how to carry your particular charge of energy better—the energy that wants to come through YOU as a human being. A different kind of energy will flow through you when you are no longer physical, but for now—ENJOY YOUR BODY!

Exercise: Letting the Charge Flow

This chapter closes with a simple exercise to open energy channels in the body.

First, just breathe, relax and notice your body sensations while lying down or sitting comfortably.

Talk to your body—ask it to receive energy in a way that is most convenient for it. One way is to nourish your body consciously with every breath you take. Let every breath be a breath of life. Notice how your body is taking in this prana, this life force.

Place your hand(s) on a part of your body where you feel nourished by the life force. These sensations could be felt as a kind of heat that begins inside the tissue and spreads outward; or you could feel tingling, goosebumps or heaviness or numbness in the affected area.

Be on the lookout for any of the body signals described in this book, especially in the eighteen hand points.

When you feel the nourishment of the life force in your body, ask it to expand and flow into another area of your body that is ready to receive it. As you continue to breathe deeply, you will notice sensations in a different part of your body. Continue to be sensitive to sensations in the original spot as well.

Let a kind of union take place between these two points in your body. Life force energy is flowing through them freely, and between them, back and forth. You are creating an energy structure to hold the life force in your body and let it flow dynamically.

Now let go and allow the life force energy to flow however it wants to, both in your body and in your surrounding energy field. Keep breathing deeply. Observe the patterns of flow. Do not spend energy worrying about where the energy is **not** flowing; rather, emphasize the points where you feel it empowering your physical tissue.

When you feel ready, ask your Oversoul (your soul perspective) to send you a wave of energy direct from its core. Breathe this energy into your cells. With each breath you are expanding your capacity to charge your electromagnetic bundle of energy.

Continue breathing in this energy until your Oversoul indicates that it's enough. You may feel the message through

one of your body signals. All you have to do is maintain
awareness of the signals—your Oversoul will handle the rest.

When you feel complete with this technique, get up slowly
and stretch.

◄○►

You may find that the level of intensity increases for you each time you
do this technique. Gradually you will get used to the idea of holding
an **unlimited amount of charge** in your body! Acceptance of your
experiences of physical intuition will make them stronger. Your beliefs
are the ground of your being that enables you to make the needed
changes in your life. Adopting an open-ended approach to life, where
there is always more to learn and experience, encourages your latent
sensitivity to emerge and blossom in the Light.

CONCLUSION

◄O►

New Directions In Growth

In Christian terms Paul wrote almost two thousand years ago that the body is the temple of the Holy Spirit. Early Christian accounts are filled with the experience of the "gifts of the Spirit" which believers channeled through the body while in a state of ecstasy. These gifts had the perceived effect of ennobling and empowering the body, so that it could do its work of "glorifying God" more effectively.

However, in the Judaeo-Christian world currents of duality drove a wedge between spirit and flesh for most of the next two millennia. Western humanity lost the perspective that the physical body is **an extension of the soul's consciousness**, as materialism spread over the entire planet. Now, as our planet is being raped and ravaged as never before, we humans are starting to recover from our Dark Night of the Soul and to realize that we have always been part of All Things. In taking care of the earth, we take care of ourselves—our body is an extension of the earth.

With an earth-centered spirituality comes a renewed respect for the body and its capabilities. One solution for environmental illness and allergies might be to get outside and work the earth! As we become part of it, we may find that it no longer rejects us, and that our symptoms disappear.

While we're working the earth, our bodies will be giving us messages that are relevant to our lives and to the lives of those around us. As our internal messages capture our attention, we may consider adopting codes of body signals such as those presented in this book. Such codes can provide a framework to develop and interpret personal sensitivity. The final outcome will be a deeper awareness of our connection to All Things, a knowledge that we are not alone and that creativity is always available to us from the depths of our personal and collective psyche. Our creative power eliminates problems and replaces them with projects and goals that motivate us from the core of our being. In other words, **we have a lot more fun!**

--<o>--

Some final remarks from my shaman Guide, He Who Walks in the Night:

Place trust in your bodies, that they will lead you to the truth. Respect them and do what they ask of you, so that you may prolong life of a high quality, that is, of great meaning. The path to truth has many twists and turns in it, as you interact with the multiplicity that you have helped create. At this time it is better to interact more forcefully with life circumstances, that you may learn from situations without becoming victims of them. Find the set of circumstances that you choose to interact with, whether it be to use them as a springboard for further growth, or to learn from them just as they are. You do not live in a vacuum, nor create in one. Your circumstances are important, since they set the stage for your growth.

Remember to take a walk in the park, or woods, or along your favorite lake. Merge with your environment—it will give you a

new perspective on yourself. One version of the creation/
destruction myth is that you find yourself, then lose yourself,
then find yourself again. The common myth is that you must go
within to find yourself, but I maintain that you can find yourself just as easily in a tree trunk or in a small animal as in meditation. It's all in your perspective: "Am I one with all things, or
am I separate?" With separation comes implosion; necessary, as
part of the cycle of creation, destruction and rebirth. But it is not
an end in itself.

Finally, see the humor in your surroundings and you will not
hold onto them as tightly. You will let inappropriate circumstances go and others take their place. See the humor in the areas
most meaningful to you—relationships, community, personal
creative expression, service to others—and watch your life circumstances change. Very quickly! Those of you who value change
for its own sake will be happy to participate in new circumstances
as you realize the benefits you can derive from the mass consciousness. Those of you who are wary of the mass consciousness, thinking of it as a polluting force, will be less successful in
changing your life circumstances to match the prevailing winds.
You do not have to blow in the same direction as the mass consciousness, but it is important to capture some current of air
outside yourself, to give you a frame of reference.

This brings us back to the body: It is naturally a built-in frame
of reference for your thoughts and feelings. As the body is allowed
to do its work, it will become more confident and will bring in
stronger messages to your awareness. You can consider your
body as a consistent tool for awareness of both inner perspectives
(your soul, your feelings) and outer ones (thoughts and feelings
of the beings around you). Body awareness acts as a check to
make sure your plans and strategies match your true intentions.

◄o►

In closing, I, Robert, wish you success and happiness as you develop your body sensitivity. As your body's intelligence becomes conscious, it will work equally with the mind to enhance your instincts and build a life of multi-dimensional richness.

BLESSED BE!

References

Coll, Francisco. *Man and the Universe*, Americana Leadership College, P.O. Box 4900, Washington, D.C. 20008, 1970.

The Foundation of *I*, Inc. *Self-I-Dentity through Ho'oponopono*, Honolulu, HI, 1989.

Fritz, Robert. *The Path of Least Resistance*, Fawcett Columbine, New York, 1989.

Murphy, Michael. *The Future of the Body*, Jeremy P. Tarcher, Inc., Los Angeles, CA, 1992.

Pearce, Joseph Chilton. *The Magical Child: Rediscovering Nature's Plan for Our Children*, Bantam Books, New York, NY, 1980.

Roberts, Jane. *Seth Speaks*, Prentice-Hall, Inc., Englewood Cliffs, NJ, 1971. *The Nature of Personal Reality*, 1974.

Sheldrake, Rupert. *The Presence of the Past: Morphic Resonance and the Habits of Nature*, Times Books, New York, NY, 1988.

Wang, Robert. *The Qabalistic Tarot*, Samuel Weiser, York Beach, ME, 1983.

Yarbro, Chelsea Quinn. *Messages from Michael*, Berkley Books, New York, NY, 1985.

About the Author

Since a near death experience in 1973, Robert Dubiel has consciously explored the paths of intuitive development. As a professional psychic counsellor, he uses telepathy to merge with the client and read the information contained in the aura (energy field). Robert's counseling can be used both as a self-awareness tool and for prediction of the probable future, helping clients see their path more clearly. Robert specializes in helping people to a greater physical awareness of their intuition through opening pathways of Light energy in the body.

In past life regression Robert uses guided imagery and suggestion to bring the client to an experience of other incarnations which affect today's life. Past life bleedthroughs can occur in the areas of relationships, phobias and health problems, cultural and historical interests. Robert helps clients to see how other lifetimes can be tapped positively or else healed and released.

An ordained minister and Reiki Master/Teacher, Robert uses laying on of hands to channel healing energy and loving compassion. He is certified to teach prospective healers Reiki as far as the Master/Teacher level.

As a rebirthing professional Robert teaches students how to breathe consciously to dissolve mental and emotional blocks, thus releasing patterns of suffering and allowing more bliss into their lives.

A native of Chicago, Robert has traveled world wide giving seminars both privately and in a group setting. He tapes private sessions both over the phone and in person. He is available for media appearances, public speaking engagements and workshops throughout the world. To promote conscious awareness of intuition in the body, Robert has written and published his book *Body Signals: Healing Through Physical Intuition*, and teaches workshops on this topic.

BODY SIGNALS

"What do chills mean?" "Why do my ears ring?"

The Body Signals system is a way to physically attune yourself to the vibrations of your Soul. This book comprehensively maps out a method to change your relationship with your body, from one of frustration to joy and satisfaction as you feel and interpret the Goose Bumps of everyday life.

The Body Signals system illustrates the truth that Spirit and Matter are one. This book provides meditations to open your spiritual sensitivity—through signals in the hands and chakras, using the body as a human pendulum for divination, developing relationships with Spirit Guides and exploring the Self through the Tree of Life of the Kabbalah. During it all, you will stay grounded as you develop a fun physical relationship with your inner child.

Order your copy today!

Fill out the order blank and mail or fax it, along with your check, money order or Visa/MC # to:

Speakers Publishing
P.O. Box 13425
Chicago Illinois 60613

email: zaRobert@gnn.com
http://members.gnn.com/zaRobert/Robert.htm

# copies	cost each	TOTAL
	$19.95 US	
1st class postage, shipping/handling	$3.00 US	

NAME: _____

ADDRESS: _____

CITY: _____ STATE: _____ ZIP: _____

COUNTRY: _____ PHONE: _____

VISA/MC: _____ EXP.: _____

Signature: _____